MY EARLY YEARS

BY THE SAME AUTHOR

My Life in Pictures

My Autobiography

MY
EARLY YEARS

Charles Chaplin

THE BODLEY HEAD
LONDON   SYDNEY
TORONTO

My Early Years is a reissue of
the early part of Charles Chaplin's
My Autobiography, first published in 1964

British Library Cataloguing
in Publication Data
Chaplin, *Sir* Charles, *b.1889*
My early years.
1. Chaplin, *Sir* Charles, b.1889
2. Moving-picture actors and actresses –
United States – Biography
I. Title
791.43′028′0924 PN2287.C5
ISBN 0–370–30230–3

© PAC Holdings, S.A. 1964
This edition © The Bodley Head Ltd 1979
All rights reserved
Printed and bound in Great Britain for
The Bodley Head Ltd
9 Bow Street, London WC2E 7AL
by William Clowes & Sons Ltd, London
Set in Monotype Plantin
First published 1964
This edition 1979

To Oona

Acknowledgments

The publishers thank copyright-holders for permission to reproduce the following photographs: Raymond Mander and Joe Mitchenson Theatre Collection for no. 5; Culver Pictures, Inc. for nos. 10 and 29; the *Radio Times* Hulton Picture Library for no. 17; the National Film Archive for nos. 19, 34, 35 and 38; Brian Love for no. 23; Simon d'Argols for nos. 24 and 31; The Museum of Modern Art, New York, for nos. 28, 30, 32 and 33; Keystone View Co. for no. 39. All photographs not specifically acknowledged are the copyright of the Chaplin Estate or of the publishers.

ILLUSTRATIONS

1. At school in Kennington, aged seven and a half, 32
2. My mother was a soubrette on the variety stage, 33
3. . . . with a fair complexion and violet-blue eyes. Sydney and I adored her, 33
4. My father, 48
5. He too was a vaudevillian, with an excellent light baritone voice, 48
6. The garret at 3 Pownall Terrace, Kennington Road, 49
7. The first floor of 287 Kennington Road, where Sydney and I lived with Louise and Father, 49
8. Where we lived, next to the slaughter-house and the pickle factory, after Mother came out of the asylum, 49
9. Lambeth Workhouse, 49
10. I played in *Sherlock Holmes* from 1901–5, in London and on tour. I remember I was very disappointed with these pictures of Billy when they were taken – I thought them extremely bad, 80
11. Among the vaudeville turns I devised for myself at the age of sixteen was an impersonation of the well-known quack, 'Dr' Walford Brodie, 81
12. I also liked to imitate the great Beerbohm Tree as Fagin in *Oliver Twist*, 81
13. Mr and Mrs Fred Karno on their houseboat at Tagg's Island, 96
14. My brother Sydney, 96
15. Five companies outside Karno's office in Camberwell leaving for the music halls in and around London, 96

16. A poster advertising Fred Karno's 'Colossal Production' of *The Football Match*, 97

17. Marie Doro in *Sherlock Holmes*, 97

18. When I was nineteen I fell in love for the first time. Hetty Kelly was fifteen, 97

19. Karno's Company hockey team. I am seated second from the left. Stan Laurel is standing behind me, 112

20. Announcing a match against Arcadia, 112

21. With Alf Reeves, his wife and Muriel Palmer on our way to America for the Karno Company, 113

22. Before my success, 113

23. . . . and after, 113

24. *The Wow-wows* opened at the Colonial Theatre, New York, on 3 October 1910, 128

25. I was still playing the drunk in *A Night in a London Club* two years later, 128

26. My manager, Alf Reeves, 128

27. Amy Minister, Alf Reeves, Muriel Palmer and Mike Asher, 129

28. Ballet Américain – the Keystone Cops, 160

29. Prosperity came to the Keystone studios after I left, 160

30. Roscoe Arbuckle, 161

31. Mabel Normand, 161

32. Ford Sterling, 161

33. Mack Sennett, 161

34. The Tramp makes his first appearance, with Mabel Normand in *Mabel's Strange Predicament*, 176

35. With Roscoe Arbuckle in *The Rounders*, 176
36. *Burlesque on Carmen*, 177
37. Edna Purviance, 177
38. G. M. Anderson, known as Bronco Billy, of the Essanay Company, who gave me my first bonus of $600, 177
39. President Freuler of the Mutual Film Company handing me a $150,000 bonus a year later, 177

PRELUDE

BEFORE Westminster Bridge was open, Kennington Road was only a bridle path. After 1750, a new road was laid down from the Bridge forming a direct link to Brighton. As a consequence Kennington Road, where I spent most of my boyhood, boasted some fine houses of architectural merit, fronted with iron grill balconies from which occupants could once have seen George IV coaching on his way to Brighton.

By the middle of the nineteenth century most of the homes had deteriorated into rooming houses and apartments. Some, however, remained inviolate and were occupied by doctors, successful merchants and vaudeville stars. On Sunday morning, along the Kennington Road one could see a smart pony and trap outside a house, ready to take a vaudevillian for a ten-mile drive as far as Norwood or Merton, stopping on the way back at the various pubs, the White Horse, the Horns and the Tankard in the Kennington Road.

As a boy of twelve, I often stood outside the Tankard watching these illustrious gentlemen alight from their equestrian outfits to enter the lounge bar, where the élite of vaudeville met, as was their custom on a Sunday to take a final 'one' before going home to the midday meal. How glamorous they were, dressed in chequered suits and grey bowlers, flashing their diamond rings and tie-pins! At two o'clock on Sunday afternoon, the pub closed and its occupants filed outside and dallied awhile before bidding each other adieu; and I would gaze fascinated and amused, for some of them swaggered with a ridiculous air.

When the last had gone his way, it was as though the sun had gone under a cloud. And I would return to a row of old derelict houses that sat back off the Kennington Road, to 3 Pownall Terrace, and mount the rickety stairs that led to our small garret. The house was depressing and the air was foul with stale slops and old clothes. This particular Sunday, Mother was seated gazing out of the window. She turned and smiled weakly. The room was stifling, a little over twelve feet square, and seemed smaller and the slanting ceiling seemed lower. The table against the wall was crowded with dirty plates and tea-cups; and in the corner, snug against the lower wall, was an old iron bed which Mother had painted white. Between the bed and the window was a small fire-grate, and at the foot of the bed an old armchair that unfolded and became a single bed upon which my brother Sydney slept. But now Sydney was away at sea.

The room was more depressing this Sunday because Mother had for some reason neglected to tidy it up. Usually she kept it clean, for she was bright, cheerful and still young, not yet thirty-seven, and could make that miserable garret glow with golden comfort. Especially on a wintry Sunday morning when she would give me my breakfast in bed and I would awaken to a tidy little room with a small fire glowing and see the steaming kettle on the hob and a haddock or a bloater by the fender being kept warm while she made toast. Mother's cheery presence, the cosiness of the room, the soft padded sound of boiling water pouring into our earthenware tea-pot while I read my weekly comic, were the pleasures of a serene Sunday morning.

But this Sunday she sat listlessly looking out of the window. For the past three days she had been sitting at that window, strangely quiet and preoccupied. I knew she was worried. Sydney was at sea and we had not heard from him in two months, and Mother's hired sewing machine with which she struggled to support us had been taken away for owing back instalments (a procedure that was not unusual). And my own contribution of five shillings weekly which I earned giving dancing lessons had suddenly ended.

I was hardly aware of a crisis because we lived in a continual crisis; and, being a boy, I dismissed our troubles with gracious

2

forgetfulness. As usual I would run home to Mother after school and do errands, empty the slops and bring up a pail of fresh water, then hurry on to the McCarthys' and spend the evening there—anything to get away from our depressing garret.

The McCarthys were old friends of Mother's whom she had known in her vaudeville days. They lived in a comfortable flat in the better part of Kennington Road, and were relatively well off by our standards. The McCarthys had a son, Wally, with whom I would play until dusk, and invariably I was invited to stay for tea. By lingering this way I had many a meal there. Occasionally Mrs McCarthy would enquire after Mother, why she had not seen her of late. And I would make some sort of excuse, for since Mother had met with adversity she seldom saw any of her theatrical friends.

Of course there were times when I would stay home, and Mother would make tea and fry bread in beef dripping, which I relished, and for an hour she would read to me, for she was an excellent reader, and I would discover the delight of Mother's company and would realise I had a better time staying home than going to the McCarthys'.

And now as I entered the room, she turned and looked reproachfully at me. I was shocked at her appearance; she was thin and haggard and her eyes had the look of someone in torment. An ineffable sadness came over me, and I was torn between an urge to stay home and keep her company, and a desire to get away from the wretchedness of it all. She looked at me apathetically. 'Why don't you run along to the McCarthys'?' she said.

I was on the verge of tears. 'Because I want to stay with you.'

She turned and looked vacantly out of the window. 'You run along to the McCarthys' and get your dinner—there's nothing here for you.'

I felt a reproach in her tone, but I closed my mind to it. 'I'll go if you want me to,' I said weakly.

She smiled wanly and stroked my head. 'Yes, yes, you run along.' And although I pleaded with her to let me stay, she insisted on my going. So I went with a feeling of guilt, leaving her sitting in that miserable garret alone, little realising that within the next few days a terrible fate awaited her.

I

I WAS born on April 16th 1889, at eight o'clock at night, in East Lane, Walworth. Soon after, we moved to West Square, St George's Road, Lambeth. According to Mother my world was a happy one. Our circumstances were moderately comfortable; we lived in three tastefully furnished rooms. One of my early recollections was that each night before Mother went to the theatre Sydney and I were lovingly tucked up in a comfortable bed and left in the care of the housemaid. In my world of three and a half years, all things were possible; if Sydney, who was four years older than I, could perform legerdemain and swallow a coin and make it come out through the back of his head, I could do the same; so I swallowed a halfpenny and Mother was obliged to send for a doctor.

Every night, after she came home from the theatre, it was her custom to leave delicacies on the table for Sydney and me to find in the morning—a slice of Neapolitan cake or candies—with the understanding that we were not to make a noise in the morning, as she usually slept late.

Mother was a soubrette on the variety stage, a *mignonne* in her late twenties, with fair complexion, violet-blue eyes and long light-brown hair that she could sit upon. Sydney and I adored our mother. Though she was not an exceptional beauty, we thought her divine-looking. Those who knew her told me in later years that she was dainty and attractive and had compelling charm. She took pride in dressing us up for Sunday excursions, Sydney in an Eton suit with long trousers and me in a blue velvet one with blue gloves to match. Such occasions were orgies of smugness, as we ambled along the Kennington Road.

London was sedate in those days. The tempo was sedate; even the horse-drawn tram-cars along Westminster Bridge Road went at a sedate pace and turned sedately on a revolving table at the terminal near the bridge. In Mother's prosperous days we also lived in Westminster Bridge Road. Its atmosphere was gay and friendly with attractive shops, restaurants and music halls. The fruit-shop on the corner facing the Bridge was a galaxy of colour, with its neatly arranged pyramids of oranges, apples, pears and bananas outside, in contrast to the solemn grey Houses of Parliament directly across the river.

This was the London of my childhood, of my moods and awakenings: memories of Lambeth in the spring; of trivial incidents and things; of riding with Mother on top of a horse-bus trying to touch passing lilac-trees—of the many coloured bus tickets, orange, blue, pink and green, that bestrewed the pavement where the trams and buses stopped—of rubicund flower-girls at the corner of Westminster Bridge, making gay *boutonnières*, their adroit fingers manipulating tinsel and quivering fern—of the humid odour of freshly watered roses that affected me with a vague sadness—of melancholy Sundays and pale-faced parents and their children escorting toy windmills and coloured balloons over Westminster Bridge; and the maternal penny steamers that softly lowered their funnels as they glided under it. From such trivia I believe my soul was born.

Then objects in our sitting-room that affected my senses: Mother's life-size painting of Nell Gwyn, which I disliked; the long-necked decanters on our sideboard, which depressed me, and the small round music-box with its enamelled surface depicting angels on clouds, which both pleased and baffled me. But my sixpenny toy chair bought from the gypsies I loved because it gave me an inordinate sense of possession.

Memories of epic moments: a visit to the Royal Aquarium,* viewing its side-shows with Mother, watching 'She', the live head of a lady smiling in flames, the sixpenny lucky dip, Mother lifting me up to a large sawdust barrel to pick a surprise packet

* A large hall which stood on the corner of Victoria Street opposite Westminster Abbey, where there were spectacular entertainments and side-shows.

which contained a candy whistle which would not blow and a toy ruby brooch. Then a visit to the Canterbury Music Hall, sitting in a red plush seat watching my father perform . . .

Now it is night and I am wrapped in a travelling rug on top of a four-in-hand coach, driving with Mother and her theatrical friends, cosseted in their gaiety and laughter as our trumpeter, with clarion braggadocio, heralds us along the Kennington Road to the rhythmic jingle of harness and the beat of horses' hoofs.

*   *   *

Then something happened! It could have been a month or a few days later—a sudden realisation that all was not well with Mother and the outside world. She had been away all the morning with a lady friend and had returned home in a state of excitement. I was playing on the floor and became conscious of intense agitation going on above me, as though I were listening from the bottom of a well. There were passionate exclamations and tears from Mother, who kept mentioning the name Armstrong—Armstrong said this, Armstrong said that, Armstrong was a brute! Her excitement was strange and intense so that I began to cry, so much so that Mother was obliged to pick me up and console me. A few years later I learned the significance of that afternoon. Mother had returned from the law courts where she had been suing my father for non-support of her children, and the case had not gone too well for her. Armstrong was my father's lawyer.

I was hardly aware of a father, and do not remember him having lived with us. He too was a vaudevillian, a quiet, brooding man with dark eyes. Mother said he looked like Napoleon. He had a light baritone voice and was considered a very fine artist. Even in those days he earned the considerable sum of forty pounds a week. The trouble was that he drank too much, which Mother said was the cause of their separation.

It was difficult for vaudevillians not to drink in those days, for alcohol was sold in all theatres, and after a performer's act

7

he was expected to go to the theatre bar and drink with the customers. Some theatres made more profit from the bar than from the box office, and a number of stars were paid large salaries not alone for their talent but because they spent most of their money at the theatre bar. Thus many an artist was ruined by drink—my father was one of them. He died of alcoholic excess at the age of thirty-seven.

Mother would tell stories about him with humour and sadness. He had a violent temper when drinking, and during one of his tantrums she ran off to Brighton with some friends, and in answer to his frantic telegram: 'What are you up to? Answer at once!' she wired back: 'Balls, parties and picnics, darling!'

Mother was the elder of two daughters. Her father, Charles Hill, an Irish cobbler, came from County Cork, Ireland. He had rosy apple cheeks, a shock of white hair and a beard like Carlyle in Whistler's portrait. He was doubled over with rheumatic gout due, he said, to sleeping in damp fields hiding from the police during the nationalist uprisings. He eventually settled in London, establishing himself in a boot-repairing business in East Lane, Walworth.

Grandma was half gypsy. This fact was the skeleton in our family cupboard. Nevertheless, Grandma bragged that her family always paid ground-rent. Her maiden name was Smith. I remember her as a bright little old lady who always greeted me effusively with baby talk. She died before I was six. She was separated from Grandpa, for what reason neither grandparent would tell. But according to Aunt Kate there was a domestic triangle in which Grandpa surprised Grandma with a lover.

To gauge the morals of our family by commonplace standards would be as erroneous as putting a thermometer in boiling water. With such genetic attributes, two pretty cobbler's daughters quickly left home and gravitated to the stage.

Aunt Kate, Mother's younger sister, was also a soubrette; but we knew little about her, for she wove in and out of our lives sporadically. She was pretty and temperamental and never got

8

along very well with Mother. Her occasional visits usually ended abruptly with acrimony at something Mother had said or done.

At eighteen Mother eloped with a middle-aged man to Africa. She often spoke of her life there; living in luxury amidst plantations, servants and saddle horses.

In her eighteenth year my brother Sydney was born. I was told he was the son of a lord and that when he reached the age of twenty-one he would inherit a fortune of two thousand pounds, which information both pleased and annoyed me.

Mother did not stay long in Africa, but returned to England and married my father. I had no knowledge of what ended the African episode, but in our extreme poverty I would reproach her for giving up such a wonderful life. She would laugh and say that she was too young to be cautious or wise.

What degree of feeling she had for my father I never knew, but whenever she spoke of him it was without bitterness, which makes me suspect she was too objective to have been deeply in love. Sometimes she would give a sympathetic account of him, and at other times talk of his drunkenness and violence. In later years, whenever angry with me she would ruefully say: 'You'll finish up in the gutter like your father.'

She had known Father before she went to Africa. They had been sweethearts, and had played together in the same Irish melodrama called *Shamus O'Brien*. At sixteen she played the leading role. While touring with this company, she met and ran off with the middle-aged lord to Africa. When she returned to England, Father took up the broken threads of their romance and they married. Three years later I was born.

What other facts besides drink were involved I do not know, but a year after my birth my parents separated. Mother did not seek alimony. Being a star in her own right, earning twenty-five pounds a week, she was well able to support herself and her children. Only when ill-fortune befell her did she seek relief; otherwise she would never have taken legal steps.

She had been having trouble with her voice. It was never

strong, and the slightest cold brought on laryngitis which lasted for weeks; but she was obliged to keep working, so that her voice grew progressively worse. She could not rely on it. In the middle of singing it would crack or suddenly disappear into a whisper, and the audience would laugh and start booing. The worry of it impaired her health and made her a nervous wreck. As a consequence, her theatrical engagements fell off until they were practically nil.

It was owing to her vocal condition that at the age of five I made my first appearance on the stage. Mother usually brought me to the theatre at night in preference to leaving me alone in rented rooms. She was playing the Canteen at Aldershot at the time, a grubby, mean theatre catering mostly to soldiers. They were a rowdy lot and wanted little excuse to deride and ridicule. To performers, Aldershot was a week of terror.

I remember standing in the wings when Mother's voice cracked and went into a whisper. The audience began to laugh and sing falsetto and to make catcalls. It was all vague and I did not quite understand what was going on. But the noise increased until Mother was obliged to walk off the stage. When she came into the wings she was very upset and argued with the stage manager who, having seen me perform before Mother's friends, said something about letting me go on in her place.

And in the turmoil I remember him leading me by the hand and, after a few explanatory words to the audience, leaving me on the stage alone. And before a glare of footlights and faces in smoke, I started to sing, accompanied by the orchestra, which fiddled about until it found my key. It was a well-known song called *Jack Jones* that went as follows:

> *Jack Jones well and known to everybody*
> *Round about the market, don't yer see,*
> *I've no fault to find with Jack at all,*
> *Not when 'e's as 'e used to be.*
> *But since 'e's had the bullion left him*
> *'E has altered for the worst,*

For to see the way he treats all his old pals
Fills me with nothing but disgust.
Each Sunday morning he reads the Telegraph,
Once he was contented with the Star.
Since Jack Jones has come into a little bit of cash,
Well, 'e don't know where 'e are.

Half-way through, a shower of money poured on to the stage.
Immediately I stopped and announced that I would pick up the
money first and sing afterwards. This caused much laughter.
The stage manager came on with a handkerchief and helped me
to gather it up. I thought he was going to keep it. This thought
was conveyed to the audience and increased their laughter,
especially when he walked off with it with me anxiously
following him. Not until he handed it to Mother did I return
and continue to sing. I was quite at home. I talked to the
audience, danced, and did several imitations including one of
Mother singing her Irish march song that went as follows:

Riley, Riley, that's the boy to beguile ye,
Riley, Riley, that's the boy for me.
In all the Army great and small,
There's none so trim and neat
As the noble Sergeant Riley
Of the gallant Eighty-eight.

And in repeating the chorus, in all innocence I imitated
Mother's voice cracking and was surprised at the impact it had
on the audience. There was laughter and cheers, then more
money-throwing; and when Mother came on the stage to
carry me off, her presence evoked tremendous applause. That
night was my first appearance on the stage and Mother's
last.

When the fates deal in human destiny, they heed neither pity
nor justice. Thus they dealt with Mother. She never regained
her voice. As autumn turns to winter, so our circumstances

turned from bad to worse. Although Mother was careful and had saved a little money, that very soon vanished, as did her jewellery and other small possessions which she pawned in order to live, hoping all the while that her voice would return.

Meanwhile from three comfortable rooms we moved into two, then into one, our belongings dwindling and the neighbourhoods into which we moved growing progressively drabber.

She turned to religion, in the hope, I suppose, that it would restore her voice. She regularly attended Christ Church in the Westminster Bridge Road, and every Sunday I was made to sit through Bach's organ music and to listen with aching impatience to the Reverend F. B. Meyer's fervent and dramatic voice echoing down the nave like shuffling feet. His orations must have been appealing, for occasionally I would catch Mother quietly wiping away a tear, which slightly embarrassed me.

Well do I remember Holy Communion on one hot summer's day, and the cool silver cup containing delicious grape-juice that passed along the congregation—and Mother's gentle restraining hand when I drank too much of it. And how relieved I was when the Reverend closed the Bible, for it meant that the sermon would soon end and they would start prayers and the final hymn.

Since Mother had joined the church she seldom saw her theatrical friends. That world had evaporated, had become only a memory. It seemed that we had always lived in wretched circumstances. The interim of one year seemed a lifetime of travail. Now we existed in cheerless twilight; jobs were hard to find and Mother, untutored in everything but the stage, was further handicapped. She was small, dainty and sensitive, fighting against terrific odds in a Victorian era in which wealth and poverty were extreme, and poorer-class women had little choice but to do menial work or to be the drudges of sweat-shops. Occasionally she obtained work nursing, but such employment was rare and of short duration. Nevertheless, she was resourceful: having made her own theatrical costumes, she was expert with her needle and able to earn a few shillings dressmaking for members of the church. But it was barely enough to support the three of us. Because of Father's drinking, his theatrical engagements became irregular, as did his payments of ten shillings a week.

Mother had now sold most of her belongings. The last thing to go was her trunk of theatrical costumes. These things she clung to in the hope that she might recover her voice and return to the stage. Occasionally, she would delve into the trunk to find something, and we would see a spangled costume or a wig and would ask her to put them on. I remember her donning a judge's cap and gown and singing in her weak voice one of her old song successes that she had written herself. The song had a bouncy two-four tempo and went as follows:

> *I'm a lady judge,*
> *And a good judge too.*
> *Judging cases fairly—*
> *They are so very rarely—*
> *I mean to teach the lawyers*
> *A thing or two,*
> *And show them just exactly*
> *What the girls can do . . .*

With amazing ease she would then break into a graceful dance and forget her dressmaking and regale us with her other song successes and perform the dances that went with them until she was breathless and exhausted. Then she would reminisce and show us some of her old playbills. One read:

> Engagement extraordinary!
> Of the dainty and talented
> Lily Harley,
> Serio-comedienne, impersonator and dancer.

She would perform before us, not only with her own vaudeville material, but with imitations of other actresses she had seen in the so-called legitimate theatre.

When narrating a play, she would act the various parts: for instance, in *The Sign of the Cross*, Mercia with divine light in her eyes going into the arena to be fed to the lions. She would imitate the high pontifical voice of Wilson Barrett proclaiming in five-inch elevated shoes—for he was a little man: 'What this Christianity is I know not. But this I do know, that if it made such women as Mercia, Rome, nay, the whole world would be all the purer for it!' . . . which she acted with a suspicion of humour, but not without an appreciation of Barrett's talent.

Her instinct was unfailing in recognising those that had genuine talent. Whether it was the actress Ellen Terry, or Joe Elvin of the music hall, she would explain their art. She knew technique instinctively and talked of theatre as only one who loved it could.

She would tell anecdotes and act them out, recounting, for instance, an episode in the life of the Emperor Napoleon: tiptoeing in his library to reach for a book and being intercepted by Marshal Ney (Mother playing both characters, but always with humour): 'Sire, allow me to get it for you. I am higher.' And Napoleon with an indignant scowl saying: 'Higher? Taller!'

She would enact Nell Gwyn, vividly describing her leaning over the palace stairs holding her baby, threatening Charles II: 'Give this child a name, or I'll dash it to the ground!' And King Charles hastily concurring: 'All right! The Duke of St Albans.'

I remember an evening in our one room in the basement at Oakley Street. I lay in bed recovering from a fever. Sydney had gone out to night school and Mother and I were alone. It was late afternoon, and she sat with her back to the window reading, acting and explaining in her inimitable way the New Testament and Christ's love and pity for the poor and for little children. Perhaps her emotion was due to my illness, but she gave the most luminous and appealing interpretation of Christ that I have ever heard or seen. She spoke of His tolerant understanding; of the woman who had sinned and was to be stoned by the mob, and of His words to them: 'He that is without sin among you, let him first cast a stone at her.'

She read into the dusk, stopping only to light the lamp, then told of the faith that Jesus inspired in the sick, that they had only to touch the hem of His garment to be healed.

She told of the hate and jealousy of the High Priests and Pharisees, and described Jesus and His arrest and His calm dignity before Pontius Pilate, who, washing his hands, said (this she acted out histrionically): 'I find no fault with this man.' She told how they stripped and scourged Him and, placing a crown of thorns on His head, mocked and spat at Him, saying: 'Hail, King of the Jews!'

As she continued tears welled up in her eyes. She told of Simon helping to carry Christ's cross and the appealing look of gratitude Jesus gave him; she told of the repentant thief, dying with Him on a cross and asking forgiveness, and of Jesus saying: 'Today shalt thou be with me in Paradise.' And from the cross looking down at His mother, saying: 'Woman, behold thy son.' And in His last dying agony crying out: 'My God, why hast Thou forsaken me?' And we both wept.

'Don't you see,' said Mother, 'how human He was; like all of us, He too suffered doubt.'

Mother had so carried me away that I wanted to die that very night and meet Jesus. But Mother was not so enthusiastic. 'Jesus wants you to live first and fulfil your destiny here,' she said. In that dark room in the basement at Oakley Street, Mother illuminated to me the kindliest light this world has ever known, which has endowed literature and the theatre with their greatest and richest themes: love, pity and humanity.

*   *   *

Living as we did in the lower strata, it was very easy to fall into the habit of not caring about our diction. But Mother always stood outside her environment and kept an alert ear on the way we talked, correcting our grammar and making us feel that we were distinguished.

As we sank further into poverty I would, in my childish ignorance, reproach her for not going back to the stage. She would smile and say that that life was false and artificial, and that in such a world one could so easily forget God. Yet whenever she talked of the theatre she would forget herself and again get carried away with enthusiasm. Some days, after reminiscing, she would fall into a long silence as she bent over her needle-work, and I would grow moody because we were no longer a part of that glamorous life. And Mother would look up and see me forlorn and would cheerfully console me.

Winter was approaching and Sydney ran out of clothes; so Mother made him a coat from her old velvet jacket. It had red and black striped sleeves, pleated at the shoulders, which Mother did her best to get rid of, but with little success. Sydney wept when he was made to wear it: 'What will the boys at school think ?'

'Who cares what people think ?' she said. 'Besides, it looks very distinguished.' Mother had such a persuasive way that Sydney to this day has never understood why he ever submitted to wearing it. But he did, and the coat and a pair of Mother's cut-down high-heeled shoes got him into many a fight at school. The boys called him 'Joseph and his coat of many colours'. And I, with a pair of Mother's red tights cut down for stockings (which looked as though they were pleated), was called 'Sir Francis Drake'.

At the depth of this dolorous period, Mother began to develop migraine headaches and was forced to give up her needlework, and for days was obliged to lie in a dark room with tea-leaf bandages over her eyes. Picasso had a blue period. We had a grey one, in which we lived on parochial charity, soup tickets

16

and relief parcels. Nevertheless, Sydney sold newspapers between school hours, and though his contribution was less than a drop in the bucket, it did give a modicum of aid. But in every crisis there is always a climax—in our case this crisis was a happy one.

One day while Mother was recovering, with a bandage still over her eyes, Sydney came bursting into the darkened room, throwing his newspapers on the bed and exclaiming: 'I've found a purse!' He handed it to Mother. When she opened it she saw a pile of silver and copper coins. Quickly she closed it, then fell back on the bed from excitement.

Sydney had been mounting buses to sell his newspapers. On top of one bus he saw a purse on an empty seat. Quickly he dropped a newspaper over it as if by accident, then picked it up and the purse with it, and hurried off the bus. Behind a bill-board, on an empty lot, he opened the purse and saw a pile of silver and copper coins. He told us that his heart leapt, and without counting the money he closed the purse and ran home.

When Mother recovered, she emptied its contents on the bed. But the purse was still heavy. There was a middle pocket! Mother opened it and saw seven golden sovereigns. Our joy was hysterical. The purse contained no address, thank God, so Mother's religious scruples were little exercised. Although a pale cast of thought was given to the owner's misfortune, it was, however, quickly dispelled by Mother's belief that God had sent it as a blessing from Heaven.

Whether Mother's illness was physical or psychological I do not know. But she recovered within a week. As soon as she was well, we went to Southend-on-Sea for a holiday, Mother outfitting us completely with new clothes.

My first sight of the sea was hypnotic. As I approached it in bright sunlight from a hilly street, it looked suspended, a live quivering monster about to fall on me. The three of us took off our shoes and paddled. The tepid sea unfurling over my insteps and around my ankles and the soft yielding sand under my feet were a revelation of delight.

What a day that was—the saffron beach, with its pink and blue pails and wooden spades, its coloured tents and umbrellas, and sailing boats hurtling gaily over laughing little waves, and up on the beach other boats resting idly on their sides, smelling of seaweed and tar—the memory of it still lingers with enchantment.

In 1957 I went back to Southend and looked in vain for the narrow, hilly street from which I had seen the sea for the first time, but there were no traces of it. At the end of the town were the remnants of what seemed a familiar fishing village with old-fashioned shop-fronts. This had vague whisperings of the past —perhaps it was the odour of seaweed and tar.

Like sand in an hour-glass our finances ran out, and hard times again pursued us. Mother sought other employment, but there was little to be found. Problems began mounting. Instalment payments were behind; consequently Mother's sewing machine was taken away. And Father's payments of ten shillings a week had completely stopped.

In desperation she sought a new solicitor, who, seeing little remuneration in the case, advised her to throw herself and her children on the support of the Lambeth Borough authorities in order to make Father pay for our support.

There was no alternative: she was burdened with two children, and in poor health; and so she decided that the three of us should enter the Lambeth workhouse.

II

ALTHOUGH we were aware of the shame of going to the workhouse, when Mother told us about it both Sydney and I thought it adventurous and a change from living in one stuffy room. But on that doleful day I didn't realise what was happening until we actually entered the workhouse gate. Then the forlorn bewilderment of it struck me; for there we were made to separate, Mother going in one direction to the women's ward and we in another to the children's.

How well I remember the poignant sadness of that first visiting day: the shock of seeing Mother enter the visiting-room garbed in workhouse clothes. How forlorn and embarrassed she looked! In one week she had aged and grown thin, but her face lit up when she saw us. Sydney and I began to weep which made Mother weep, and large tears began to run down her cheeks. Eventually she regained her composure and we sat together on a rough bench, our hands in her lap while she gently patted them. She smiled at our cropped heads and stroked them consolingly, telling us that we would soon all be together again. From her apron she produced a bag of coconut candy which she had bought at the workhouse store with her earnings from crocheting lace cuffs for one of the nurses. After we parted, Sydney kept dolefully repeating how she had aged.

*   *   *

Sydney and I quickly adapted ourselves to workhouse life, but in an overcast sadness. I remember little of incident, but the midday meal at a long table with other children was a warm and expectant affair. It was presided over by an inmate of the workhouse, an old gentleman of about seventy-five, with a dignified countenance, a thin white beard and sad eyes. He elected me to sit next to him because I was the youngest and, until they cropped my head, had the curliest hair. He called me his 'tiger' and said that when I grew bigger I would wear a top hat with a cockade and would sit at the back of his carriage with my arms folded. This honour made me very fond of him. But a day or so later a younger boy appeared on the scene with curlier hair than I had and took my place beside the old gentleman, because, as he whimsically explained, a younger and curlier-headed boy always took precedence.

After three weeks we were transferred from Lambeth Workhouse to the Hanwell Schools for Orphans and Destitute Children about twelve miles out of London. It was an adventurous drive in a horse-drawn bakery van, and rather a happy one under the circumstances, for the country surrounding Hanwell was beautiful in those days, with lanes of horse-chestnut trees, ripening wheat-fields and heavy-laden orchards, and ever since the rich, aromatic smell after rain in the country has always reminded me of Hanwell.

On arriving we were delivered to the approbation ward and put under medical and mental observation before entering the school proper; the reason was that amongst three to four hundred boys a subnormal child or a sick one would be unhealthy for the school as well as being in an unhappy situation himself.

The first few days I was lost and miserable, for at the workhouse I always felt that Mother was near, which was comforting, but at Hanwell we seemed miles apart. Sydney and I graduated from the approbation ward to the school proper, where we were separated, Sydney going with the big boys and I with the infants. We slept in different ward blocks, so we seldom saw each other. I was a little over six years old and alone, which made me feel quite abject; especially on a summer's evening at bed-time during prayers, when, kneeling with twenty other little boys in the centre of the ward in our night-shirts, I would look out of the oblong windows at the deepening sunset and the undulating hills, and feel alien to it all as we sang in throaty off-key voices:

Abide with me; fast falls the eventide;
The darkness deepens: Lord, with me abide;
When other helpers fail, and comforts flee,
Help of the helpless, O, abide with me.

It was then that I felt utterly dejected. Although I did not understand the hymn, the tune and the twilight increased my sadness.

But, to our happy surprise, within two months Mother had arranged for our discharge, and we were dispatched again to London and the Lambeth workhouse. Mother was at the gate dressed in her own clothes, waiting for us. She had applied for a discharge only because she wanted to spend the day with her children, intending, after a few hours outside together, to return the same day; Mother being an inmate of the workhouse, this ruse was her only means to be with us.

Before we entered our private clothes had been taken from us and steamed; now they were returned unpressed. Mother, Sydney and I looked a crumpled sight as we ambled out through the workhouse gates. It was early morning and we had nowhere to go, so we walked to Kennington Park, which was about a mile away. Sydney had ninepence tied up in a handkerchief, so we bought half a pound of black cherries and spent the morning in Kennington Park, sitting on a bench eating them. Sydney crumpled a sheet of newspaper and wrapped some string around it and for a while the three of us played catch-ball. At noon we went to a coffee-shop and spent the rest of our money on a twopenny tea-cake, a penny bloater and two halfpenny cups of tea, which we shared between us. Afterwards we returned to the park where Sydney and I played again while Mother sat crocheting.

In the afternoon we made our way back to the workhouse. As Mother said with levity: 'We'll be just in time for tea.' The authorities were most indignant, because it meant going through the same procedure of having our clothes steamed and Sydney and I spending more time at the workhouse before returning to Hanwell, which of course gave us an opportunity of seeing Mother again.

But this time we stayed at Hanwell for almost a year—a most formative year, in which I started schooling and was taught to write my name 'Chaplin'. The word fascinated me and looked like me, I thought.

Hanwell School was divided in two, a department for boys and one for girls. On Saturday afternoon the bath-house was reserved for infants, who were bathed by the older girls. This, of course, 'was before I was seven, and a squeamish modesty attended these occasions; having to submit to the ignominy of a young girl of fourteen manipulating a facecloth all over my person was my first conscious embarrassment.

At the age of seven I was transferred from the infants' to the older boys' department, where ages ranged from seven to fourteen. Now I was eligible to participate in all the grown-up functions, the drills and exercises and the regular walks we took outside the school twice a week.

Although at Hanwell we were well looked after, it was a forlorn existence. Sadness was in the air; it was in those country lanes through which we walked, a hundred of us two abreast. How I disliked those walks, and the villages through which we passed, the locals staring at us! We were known as inmates of the 'booby hatch', a slang term for workhouse.

The boys' playground was approximately an acre, paved with slab-stones. Surrounding it were one-storey brick buildings, used for offices, store-rooms, a doctor's dispensary, a dentist's office and a wardrobe for boys' clothing. In the darkest corner of the yard was an empty room, and recently confined there was a boy of fourteen, a desperate character according to the other boys. He had attempted to escape from the school by climbing out of a second-storey window and up on to the roof, defying the officials by throwing missiles and horse-chestnuts at them as they climbed after him. This happened after we infants were

22

asleep: we were given an awed account of it by the older boys the next morning.

For major offences of this nature, punishment took place every Friday in the large gymnasium, a gloomy hall about sixty feet by forty with a high roof, and, on the side, climbing ropes running up to girders. On Friday morning two to three hundred boys, ranging in age from seven to fourteen years, marched in and lined up in military fashion, forming three sides of a square. The far end was the fourth side, where, behind a long school desk the length of an Army mess-table, stood the miscreants waiting for trial and punishment. On the right and in front of the desk was an easel with wrist-straps dangling, and from the frame a birch hung ominously.

For minor offences, a boy was laid across the long desk, face downwards, feet strapped and held by a sergeant, then another sergeant pulled the boy's shirt out of his trousers and over his head, then pulled his trousers tight.

Captain Hindrum, a retired Navy man weighing about two hundred pounds, with one hand behind him, the other holding a cane as thick as a man's thumb and about four feet long, stood poised, measuring it across the boy's buttocks. Then slowly and dramatically he would lift it high and with a swish bring it down across the boy's bottom. The spectacle was terrifying, and invariably a boy would fall out of rank in a faint.

The minimum number of strokes was three and the maximum six. If a culprit received more than three, his cries were appalling. Sometimes he was ominously silent, or had fainted. The strokes were paralysing, so that the victim had to be carried to one side and laid on a gymnasium mattress, where he was left to writhe and wriggle for at least ten minutes before the pain subsided, leaving three pink welts as wide as a washerwoman's finger across his bottom.

The birch was different. After three strokes, the boy was supported by two sergeants and taken to the surgery for treatment.

Boys would advise you not to deny a charge, even if innocent, because, if proved guilty, you would get the maximum. Usually, boys were not articulate enough to declare their innocence.

I was now seven and in the big boys' section. I remember witnessing my first flogging, standing in silence, my heart thumping as the officials entered. Behind the desk was the desperado who had tried to escape from the school. We could hardly see more than his head and shoulders over the desk, he looked so small. He had a thin, angular face and large eyes.

The headmaster solemnly read the charges and demanded: 'Guilty or not guilty?'

Our desperado would not answer, but stared defiantly in front of him; he was thereupon led to the easel, and being small, he was made to stand on a soap-box so that his wrists could be strapped. He received three strokes with the birch and was led away to the surgery for treatment.

On Thursdays, a bugle sounded in the playground and we would all stop playing, taking a frozen position like statues, while Captain Hindrum, through a megaphone, announced the names of those who were to report for punishment on Friday.

One Thursday, to my astonishment I heard my name called. I could not imagine what I had done. Yet for some unaccountable reason I was thrilled—perhaps because I was the centre of a drama. On the day of the trial, I stepped forward. Said the headmaster: 'You are charged with setting fire to the dykes' (the lavatory).

This was not true. Some boys had lit a few bits of paper on the stone floor and while they were burning I came in to use the lavatory, but I had played no part in that fire.

'Are you guilty or not guilty?' he asked.

Nervous and impelled by a force beyond my control, I blurted out: 'Guilty.' I felt neither resentment nor injustice but a sense of frightening adventure as they led me to the desk and administered three strokes across my bottom. The pain was so excruciating that it took away my breath; but I did not cry out, and, although paralysed with pain and carried to the mattress to recover, I felt valiantly triumphant.

As Sydney was working in the kitchen, he had not known about it until punishment day, when he was marched into the gymnasium with the others and to his shocked amazement saw my head peering over the desk. He told me afterwards that when he saw me receiving three strokes he wept with rage.

A younger brother referred to his older brother as 'my young 'un', which made him feel proud and gave him a little security. So occasionally I saw 'my young 'un', Sydney, as I was leaving the dining-room. As he worked in the kitchen, he would surreptitiously hand me a sliced bread roll with a thick lump of butter pressed between, and I would smuggle it under my jersey and share it with another boy—not that we were hungry, but the generous lump of butter was an exceptional luxury. But these delicacies were not to continue, for Sydney left Hanwell to join the *Exmouth* training ship.

At the age of eleven a workhouse boy had the choice of joining the Army or the Navy. If the Navy, he was sent to the *Exmouth*. Of course, it was not obligatory, but Sydney wanted to make a career of the sea. So that left me alone at Hanwell.

*   *   *

Hair is vitally personal to children. They weep vigorously when it is cut for the first time; no matter how it grows, bushy, straight or curly, they feel they are being shorn of a part of their personality.

There had been an epidemic of ringworm at Hanwell and, as it is most contagious, those infected were dispatched to the isolation ward on the first floor overlooking the playground. Often we would look up at the windows and see those wretched boys looking wistfully down at us, their heads shaved all over and stained brown with iodine. They were a hideous sight and we would look up at them with loathing.

25

Thus when a nurse stopped abruptly behind me in the dining-room and parted the top of my hair and announced: 'Ringworm!' I was thrown into paroxysms of weeping.

The treatment took weeks and seemed like an eternity. My head was shaved and iodined and I wore a handkerchief tied around it like a cotton-picker. But one thing I would not do was to look out of the window at the boys below, for I knew in what contempt they held us.

During my incarceration Mother visited me. She had in some way managed to leave the workhouse and was making an effort to establish a home for us. Her presence was like a bouquet of flowers; she looked so fresh and lovely that I felt ashamed of my unkempt appearance and my shaved iodined head.

'You must excuse his dirty face,' said the nurse.

Mother laughed, and how well I remember her endearing words as she hugged and kissed me: 'With all thy dirt I love thee still.'

Soon afterwards, Sydney left the *Exmouth* and I left Hanwell and we joined Mother again. She took a room at the back of Kennington Park and for a while she was able to support us. But it was not long before we were back in the workhouse again. The circumstances that led up to our return were something to do with Mother's difficulty in finding employment and Father's slump in his theatrical engagements. In that brief interlude we kept moving from one back-room to another; it was like a game of draughts—the last move was back to the workhouse.

Living in a different parish, we were sent to a different workhouse, and from there to Norwood Schools, which was more sombre than Hanwell; leaves darker and trees taller. Perhaps the countryside had more grandeur, but the atmosphere was joyless.

One day, while Sydney was playing football, two nurses called him out of the game and told him that Mother had gone insane and had been sent to Cane Hill lunatic asylum. When

Sydney heard the news he showed no reaction but went back and continued playing football. But after the game he stole away by himself and wept.

When he told me I could not believe it. I did not cry, but a baffling despair overcame me. Why had she done this? Mother, so light-hearted and gay, how could she go insane? Vaguely I felt that she had deliberately escaped from her mind and had deserted us. In my despair I had visions of her looking pathetically at me, drifting away into a void.

We heard the news officially a week later; we also heard that the court decreed that Father must take over the custody of Sydney and me. The prospect of living with Father was exciting. I had seen him only twice in my life, on the stage, and once when passing a house in the Kennington Road, as he was coming down the front garden path with a lady. I had paused and watched him, knowing instinctively that he was my father. He beckoned me to him and asked my name. Sensing the drama of the situation, I had feigned innocence and said: 'Charlie Chaplin'. Then he glanced knowingly at the lady, felt in his pocket and gave me half a crown, and without further ado I ran straight home and told Mother that I had met my father.

And now we were going to live with him. Whatever happened, Kennington Road was familiar and not strange and sombre like Norwood.

The officials drove us in the bread van to 287 Kennington Road, the house where I had seen my father walking down the garden path. The door was opened by the lady who had been with him at the time. She was dissipated and morose-looking, yet attractive, tall and shapely, with full lips and sad, doe-like eyes; her age could have been thirty. Her name was Louise. It appeared that Mr Chaplin was not at home, but after the usual formalities and the signing of papers the official left us in charge of Louise, who led us upstairs to the first landing into the front sitting-room. A small boy was playing on the

27

floor as we entered, a most beautiful child of four with large dark eyes and rich brown curly hair: it was Louise's son—my half-brother.

The family lived in two rooms and, although the front room had large windows, the light filtered in as if from under water. Everything looked as sad as Louise; the wallpaper looked sad, the horse-hair furniture looked sad, and the stuffed pike in a glass case that had swallowed another pike as large as itself—the head sticking out of its mouth—looked gruesomely sad.

In the back room she had put an extra bed for Sydney and me to sleep on, but it was too small. Sydney suggested sleeping on the sofa in the sitting-room. 'You'll sleep where you're told to,' said Louise. This caused an embarrassing silence as we walked back into the living-room.

Our reception was not an enthusiastic one, and no wonder. Sydney and I had been suddenly thrust upon her, and moreover we were the offspring of Father's estranged wife.

We both sat mutely watching her preparing the table for something to eat. 'Here,' she said to Sydney, 'you can make yourself useful and fill the coal-scuttle. And you,' she said, turning to me, 'go to the cook-shop next to the White Hart and get a shilling's worth of corned beef.'

I was only too pleased to leave her presence and the whole atmosphere, for a lurking fear was growing within me and I began to wish we were back at Norwood.

Father arrived home later and greeted us kindly. He fascinated me. At meals I watched every move he made, the way he ate and the way he held his knife as though it were a pen when cutting his meat. And for years I copied him.

When Louise told of Sydney's complaining about the small bed, Father suggested that Sydney should sleep on the sitting-room sofa. This victory of Sydney's aroused Louise's antagonism and she never forgave him. She continually complained to Father about him. Although Louise was morose and disagreeable, she never once struck me or even threatened to, but the fact that she disliked Sydney held me in fear and dread of her. She drank a great deal, and this exaggerated my fear. There was something frighteningly irresponsible about her when she was drunk; she would smile with amusement at her little boy with his beautiful angelic face, who would swear at her and use vile language. For some reason, I never had contact with the child. Although he was my half-brother, I don't remember ever having exchanged a word with him—of course I was almost four years older than he. Sometimes when drinking Louise would sit and brood and I would be in a state of dread. But Sydney paid little attention to her; he seldom came home until late at night. I was made to come home directly after school and run errands and do odd jobs.

Louise sent us to the Kennington Road School, which was a bleak divertissement, for the presence of other children made me feel less isolated. Saturday was a half-holiday, but I never looked forward to it because it meant going home and scrubbing floors and cleaning knives, and on that day Louise invariably started drinking. While I was cleaning the knives, she would sit with a lady friend, drinking and growing bitterly morose, complaining quite audibly to her friend of having to look after Sydney and me and of the injustice imposed upon her. I remember her saying: 'This one's all right' (indicating me), 'but the other's a little swine and should be sent to a reformatory—what's more, he's not even Charlie's son.' This reviling of Sydney frightened and depressed me and I would go unhappily to bed and lie fretfully awake. I was not yet eight years old, but those days were the longest and saddest of my life.

Sometimes on a Saturday night, feeling deeply despondent, I would hear the lively music of a concertina passing by the back bedroom window, playing a highland march, accompanied by rowdy youths and giggling coster girls. The vigour and vitality of it seemed ruthlessly indifferent to my unhappiness, yet as the music grew fainter into the distance, I would regret it leaving. Sometimes a street-crier would pass: one in particular came by every night who seemed to be shouting 'Rule Britannia', terminating it with a grunt, but he was actually selling oysters. From the pub, three doors away, I could hear the customers at closing time, singing drunks, bawling out a maudlin, dreary song that was popular in those days:

> *For old times' sake don't let our enmity live,*
> *For old times' sake say you'll forget and forgive.*
> *Life's too short to quarrel,*
> *Hearts are too precious to break.*
> *Shake hands and let us be friends*
> *For old times' sake.*

I never appreciated the sentiment, but it seemed an appropriate accompaniment to my unhappy circumstances, and lulled me to sleep.

When Sydney came in late, which seemed always, he raided the larder before going to bed. This infuriated Louise, and one night when she had been drinking she came into the room and ripped the bedclothes off him and told him to get out. But Sydney was prepared for her. Quickly he reached under his pillow and whipped out a stiletto, a long button-hook which he had sharpened to a point.

'Come near me,' he said, 'and I'll stick this in you!'

She reared back, startled. 'Why, the bloody young sod!—he's going to murder me!'

'Yes,' said Sydney, dramatically, 'I'll murder you!'

'You wait till Mr Chaplin comes home!'

But Mr Chaplin seldom came home. However, I remember one Saturday night when Louise and Father had been drinking, and for some reason we were all sitting with the landlady and her husband in their front-room parlour on the ground floor. Under the incandescent light Father looked ghastly pale, and in an ugly mood was mumbling to himself. Suddenly he reached into his pocket, pulled out a handful of money and threw it violently to the floor, scattering gold and silver coins in all directions. The effect was surrealistic. No one moved. The landlady sat glum, but I caught her roving eye following a golden sovereign rolling to a far corner under a chair; my eye also followed it. Still no one moved, so I thought I had better start picking it up; the landlady and the others followed suit, picking up the rest of the money, careful to make their actions overt before Father's menacing eyes.

One Saturday, after school, I came home to find no one there. Sydney, as usual, was away all day playing football and the landlady said Louise and her son had been out since early morning. At first I was relieved, for it meant that I did not have to scrub floors and clean knives. I waited until long after lunchtime, then began to get anxious. Perhaps they had deserted me. As the afternoon wore on, I began to miss them. What had happened? The room looked grim and unyielding and its emptiness frightened me. I also began to get hungry, so I looked in the larder, but no food was there. I could stand the gaping emptiness no longer, so in desolation I went out, spending the afternoon visiting nearby market places. I wandered through Lambeth Walk and the Cut, looking hungrily into cook-shop windows at the tantalising steaming roast joints of beef and pork, and the golden-brown potatoes soaked in gravy. For hours I watched the quacks selling their wares. The distraction soothed me and for a while I forgot my plight and hunger.

When I returned, it was night; I knocked at the door, but no one answered. Everyone was out. Wearily I walked to the corner of Kennington Cross and sat on the kerb near the house to keep an eye on it in case someone returned. I was tired and miserable, and wondered where Sydney was. It was approaching midnight and Kennington Cross was deserted but for one or two stragglers. All the lights of the shops began going out except those of the chemist and the public houses, then I felt wretched.

Suddenly there was music. Rapturous! It came from the vestibule of the White Hart corner pub, and resounded brilliantly in the empty square. The tune was *The Honeysuckle and the Bee*, played with radiant virtuosity on a harmonium and clarinet. I had never been conscious of melody before, but this one was beautiful and lyrical, so blithe and gay, so warm and reassuring. I forgot my despair and crossed the road to where the musicians were. The harmonium-player was blind, with scarred sockets where the eyes had been; and a besotted, embittered face played the clarinet.

It was all over too soon and their exit left the night even sadder. Weak and tired, I crossed the road towards the house, not caring whether anyone came home or not. All I wanted was to get to bed. Then dimly I saw someone going up the garden path towards the house. It was Louise—and her little son running ahead of her. I was shocked to see that she was limping exaggeratedly and leaning extremely to one side. At first I thought she had been in an accident and had hurt her leg, then I realised she was very drunk. I had never seen a lopsided drunk before. In her condition I thought it best to keep out of her way, so I waited until she had let herself in. A few moments later the landlady came home and I went in with her. As I crept up the darkened stairs, hoping to get to bed unnoticed, Louise staggered out on to the landing.

'Where the hell do you think you're going?' she said. 'This is not your home.'

I stood motionless.

'You're not sleeping here tonight. I've had enough of all of you; get out! You and your brother! Let your father take care of you.'

Without hesitation, I turned and went downstairs and out of the house. I was no longer tired; I had got my second wind. I had heard that Father patronised the Queen's Head pub in the Prince's Road, about half a mile away, so I made my way in that direction, hoping to find him there. But soon I saw his shadowy figure coming towards me, outlined against the street-lamp.

1. At school in Kennington, aged seven and a half

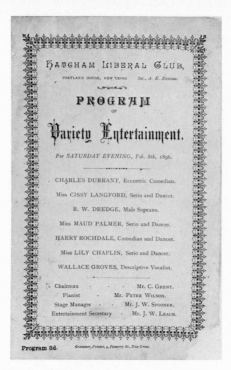

2. My mother was a soubrette on the variety stage

3. . . . with a fair complexion and violet-blue eyes.
Sydney and I adored her

'She won't let me in,' I whimpered, 'and I think she's been drinking.'

As we walked towards the house he also staggered. 'I'm not sober myself,' he said.

I tried to reassure him that he was.

'No, I'm drunk,' he muttered, remorsefully.

He opened the door of the sitting-room and stood there silent and menacing, looking at Louise. She was standing by the fireplace, holding on to the mantelpiece, swaying.

'Why didn't you let him in?' he said.

She looked at him bewildered, then mumbled: 'You too can go to hell—all of you!'

Suddenly he picked up a heavy clothes-brush from the sideboard and like a flash threw it violently, the back of it hitting her flat on the side of her face. Her eyes closed, then she collapsed unconscious with a thud to the floor as though she welcomed oblivion.

I was shocked at Father's action; such violence made me lose respect for him. As to what happened afterwards, my memory is vague. I believe Sydney came in later and Father saw us both to bed, then left the house.

I learned that Father and Louise had quarrelled that morning because he had left her to spend the day with his brother, Spencer Chaplin, who owned several public houses round and about Lambeth. Being sensitive of her position, Louise disliked visiting the Spencer Chaplins, so Father went alone, and as a revenge Louise spent the day elsewhere.

She loved Father. Even though very young I could see it in her glance the night she stood by the fireplace, bewildered and hurt by his neglect. And I am sure he loved her. I saw many occasions of it. There were times when he was charming and tender and would kiss her good-night before leaving for the theatre. And on a Sunday morning, when he had not been drinking, he would breakfast with us and tell Louise about the vaudeville acts that were working with him, and have us all enthralled. I would watch him like a hawk, absorbing every action. In a playful mood, he once wrapped a towel round his head and chased his little son around the table, saying: 'I'm King Turkey Rhubarb.'

About eight o'clock in the evening, before departing for the theatre, he would swallow six raw eggs in port wine, rarely eating solid food. That was all that sustained him day after day. He seldom came home, and, if he did, it was to sleep off his drinking.

One day Louise received a visit from the Society for the Prevention of Cruelty to Children, and she was most indignant about it. They came because the police had reported finding Sydney and me asleep at three o'clock in the morning by a watchman's fire. It was a night that Louise had shut us both out, and the police had made her open the door and let us in.

A few days later, however, while Father was playing in the provinces, Louise received a letter announcing that Mother had left the asylum. A day or two later the landlady came up and announced that there was a lady at the front door to call for Sydney and Charlie. 'There's your mother,' said Louise. There was a momentary confusion. Then Sydney leaped downstairs into her arms, I following. It was the same sweet, smiling Mother who affectionately embraced us.

Louise and Mother were too embarrassed to meet, so Mother waited at the front door while Sydney and I collected our things. There was no umbrage or ill-feeling on either side—in fact, Louise's manner was most agreeable, even to Sydney when she bade him goodbye.

*   *   *

Mother had taken a room in one of the back streets behind Kennington Cross near Hayward's pickle factory, and the acid smell would start up every afternoon. But the room was cheap and we were all together again. Mother's health was excellent, and the thought that she had been ill never entered our heads.

How we lived through this period I have not the remotest idea. Nonetheless, I remember no undue hardships or insoluble problems. Father's payments of ten shillings a week were almost regular, and, of course, Mother took up her needlework again and renewed her contact with the church.

An incident stands out at that period. At the end of our street was a slaughter-house, and sheep would pass our house on their way to be butchered. I remember one escaped and ran down the street to the amusement of onlookers. Some tried to grab it and others tripped over themselves. I had giggled with delight at its lambent capering and panic, it seemed so comic. But when it was caught and carried back into the slaughter-house, the reality of the tragedy came over me and I ran indoors, screaming and weeping to Mother: 'They're going to kill it! They're going to kill it!' That stark, spring afternoon and that comedy chase stayed with me for days; and I wonder if that episode did not establish the premise of my future films—the combination of the tragic and the comic.

School was now the beginning of new horizons: history, poetry and science. But some of the subjects were prosaic and dull, especially arithmetic: its addition and subtraction gave an image of a clerk and a cash register, its use, at best, a protection against being short-changed.

History was a record of wickedness and violence, a continual succession of regicides and kings murdering their wives, brothers and nephews; geography merely maps; poetry nothing more than exercising memory. Education bewildered me with knowledge and facts in which I was only mildly interested.

If only someone had used salesmanship, had read a stimulating preface to each study that could have titillated my mind, infused me with fancy instead of facts, amused and intrigued me with the legerdemain of numbers, romanticised maps, given me a point of view about history and taught me the music of poetry, I might have become a scholar.

Since Mother had returned to us she had begun to stimulate my interest in the theatre again. She imbued me with the feeling that I had some sort of talent. But it was not until those weeks before Christmas when the school put on its cantata *Cinderella* that I felt an urge to express all that Mother had taught me. For some reason I was not selected to play in it, and inwardly I was envious and felt that I was better able to play in the cantata than those who had been chosen. I was critical of the dull, unimaginative way the boys played their parts. The Ugly Sisters had no zest or comic spirit. They spoke their lines eruditely with a schoolboy inflection and an embarrassing falsetto emphasis. How I would have loved to play one of the Ugly Sisters, with the tutoring Mother could have given me! I was, however, captivated by the girl who played Cinderella. She was beautiful, refined, aged about fourteen, and I was secretly in love with her. But she was beyond my reach both socially and in years.

When I saw the cantata, I thought it dismal but for the beauty of the girl, which left me a little sad. Little did I realise, however, the glorious triumph I was to enjoy two months later when I was brought before each class and made to recite *Miss Priscilla's Cat*. It was a comedy recitation Mother had seen outside a newspaper shop and thought so funny that she copied it from the window and brought it home. During a recess in class, I recited it to one of the boys. Mr Reid, our school-teacher, looked up from his work and was so amused that when the class assembled he made me recite it to them and they were thrown into gales of laughter. As a result of this my fame spread, and the following day I was brought before every classroom in the school, both boys and girls, and made to recite it.

Although I had performed and deputised for Mother in front of an audience at the age of five, this was actually my first conscious taste of glamour. School became exciting. From having been an obscure and shy little boy I became the centre of interest of both the teachers and the children. It even improved my studies. But my education was to be interrupted when I left to join a troupe of clog dancers, the Eight Lancashire Lads.

III

FATHER knew Mr Jackson, who ran the troupe, and convinced Mother that it would be a good start for me to make a career on the stage and at the same time help her economically: I would get board and lodging and Mother would get half a crown a week. She was dubious at first until she met Mr Jackson and his family, then she accepted.

Mr Jackson was in his middle fifties. He had been a school-teacher in Lancashire and had raised a family of three boys and a girl, who were all a part of the Eight Lancashire Lads. He was a devout Roman Catholic and after his first wife died had consulted his children about marrying again. His second wife was a little older than himself, and he would piously tell us how he came to marry her. He had advertised for a wife in one of the newspapers and had received over three hundred letters. After praying for guidance he had opened only one, and that was from Mrs Jackson. She too had been a school-teacher and, as if in answer to his prayer, was also a Catholic.

Mrs Jackson was not blessed with abundant good looks, nor was she a voluptuary in any sense of the word. As I remember her she had a gaunt, skull-like, pale face with manifold wrinkles —due, perhaps, to having presented Mr Jackson with a baby boy rather late in life. Nevertheless, she was a loyal and dutiful wife and, although still nursing her son at the breast, worked hard at helping with the management of the troupe.

When she told her side of the romance, it varied slightly from that of Mr Jackson. They had exchanged letters, but neither one had seen the other until the day of the wedding. And in their first interview alone in the sitting-room while the family waited in another room, Mr Jackson said: 'You're all that I desire,' and she avowed the same. In concluding the story to us boys, she would primly say: 'But I didn't expect to be the immediate mother of eight children.'

The three sons' ages ranged from twelve to sixteen, and the daughter was nine, with hair cut like a boy in order to pass as one in the troupe.

Each Sunday, everyone attended Catholic church but me. Being the only Protestant, I was lonely, so occasionally I went with them. Had it not been for deference to Mother's religious scruples, I could easily have been won over to Catholicism, for I liked the mysticism of it and the little home-made altars with plaster Virgin Marys adorned with flowers and lighted candles which the boys put up in a corner of the bedroom, and to which they would genuflect every time they passed.

After practising six weeks I was eligible to dance with the troupe. But now that I was past eight years old I had lost my assurance and confronting the audience for the first time gave me stage fright. I could hardly move my legs. It was weeks before I could solo dance as the rest of them did.

I was not particularly enamoured with being just a clog dancer in a troupe of eight lads. Like the rest of them I was ambitious to do a single act, not only because it meant more money but because I instinctively felt it to be more gratifying than just dancing. I would have liked to be a boy comedian— but that would have required nerve, to stand on the stage alone. Nevertheless, my first impulse to do something other than dance was to be funny. My ideal was a double act, two boys dressed as comedy tramps. I told it to one of the other boys and we decided to become partners. It became our cherished dream. We would call ourselves 'Bristol and Chaplin, the Millionaire Tramps', and would wear tramp whiskers and big diamond rings. It embraced every aspect of what we thought would be funny and profitable, but, alas, it never materialised.

Audiences liked the Eight Lancashire Lads because, as Mr Jackson said, we were so unlike theatrical children. It was his boast that we never wore grease-paint and that our rosy cheeks were natural. If some of us looked a little pale before going on, he would tell us to pinch our cheeks. But in London, after working two or three music halls a night, we would occasionally forget and look a little weary and bored as we stood on the stage, until we caught sight of Mr Jackson in the wings, grinning emphatically and pointing to his face, which had an electrifying effect of making us suddenly break into sparkling grins.

When touring the provinces we went to a school for the week in each town, which did little to further my education.

At Christmas time we were engaged to play cats and dogs in a Cinderella pantomime at the London Hippodrome. In those days, it was a new theatre, a combination of vaudeville and circus, elaborately decorated and quite sensational. The floor of the ring sank and flooded with water and elaborate ballets were contrived. Row after row of pretty girls in shining armour would march in and disappear completely under water. As the last line submerged, Marceline, the great French clown, dressed in sloppy evening dress and opera hat, would enter with a fishing rod, sit on a camp stool, open a large jewel-case, bait his hook with a diamond necklace, then cast it into the water. After a while he would 'chum' with smaller jewellery, throwing in a few bracelets, eventually emptying in the whole jewel-case. Suddenly he would get a bite and throw himself into paroxysms of comic gyrations struggling with the rod, and eventually pulling out of the water a small trained poodle dog, who copied everything Marceline did: if he sat down, the dog sat down; if he stood on his head, the dog did likewise.

Marceline's comedy was droll and charming and London went wild over him. In the kitchen scene I was given a little comedy bit to do with Marceline. I was a cat, and Marceline would back away from a dog and fall over my back while I drank milk. He always complained that I did not arch my back enough to break his fall. I wore a cat-mask which had a look of surprise, and during the first matinée for children I went up to the rear end of a dog and began to sniff. When the audience laughed, I turned and looked surprised at them, pulling a string which winked a staring eye. After several sniffs and winks

the house-manager came bounding back stage, waving frantic-
ally in the wings. But I carried on. After smelling the dog, I
smelt the proscenium, then I lifted my leg. The audience
roared—possibly because the gesture was uncatlike. Eventually the manager caught my eye and I capered off to great
applause. 'Never do that again!' he said, breathlessly. 'You'll
have the Lord Chamberlain close down the theatre!'

Cinderella was a great success, and although Marceline had
little to do with plot or story, he was the star attraction. Years
later Marceline went to the New York Hippodrome, where he
was also a sensation. But when the Hippodrome abolished the
circus ring, Marceline was soon forgotten.

In 1918, or thereabouts, Ringling Brothers' three-ring circus
came to Los Angeles, and Marceline was with them. I expected
that he would be featured, but I was shocked to find him just
one of many clowns that ran around the enormous ring—a
great artist lost in the vulgar extravagance of a three-ring
circus.

I went to his dressing-room afterwards and made myself
known, reminding him that I had played Cat at the London
Hippodrome with him. But he reacted apathetically. Even under
his clown make-up he looked sullen and seemed in a melancholy
torpor.

A year later in New York he committed suicide. A small para-
graph in the papers stated that an occupant living in the same
house had heard a shot and had found Marceline lying on the
floor with a pistol in his hand and a record still turning, playing
Moonlight and Roses.

Many famous English comedians committed suicide. T. E.
Dunville, an excellent funny man, overheard someone say as he
entered a saloon bar: 'That fellow's through.' The same day he
shot himself by the River Thames.

Mark Sheridan, one of England's foremost comedians, shot
himself in a public park in Glasgow because he had not gone
over well with the Glasgow audience.

41

Frank Coyne, with whom we played on the same bill, was a gay, bouncy type of comedian, famous for his breezy song:

> *You won't catch me on the gee-gee's back again,*
> *It's not the kind of horse that I can ride on.*
> *The only horse I know that I can ride*
> *Is the one the missus dries the clothes on!*

Off stage he was pleasant and always smiling. But one afternoon, after planning to take a drive with his wife in their pony and trap, he forgot something and told her to wait while he went upstairs. After twenty minutes she went up to see what was causing the delay, and found him in the bathroom on the floor in a pool of blood, a razor in his hand—he had cut his throat, almost decapitating himself.

Of the many artists I saw as a child, those who impressed me the most were not always the successful ones but those with unique personalities off stage. Zarmo, the comedy tramp juggler, was a disciplinarian who practised his juggling for hours every morning as soon as the theatre opened. We could see him back stage balancing a billiard cue on his chin and throwing a billiard ball up and catching it on the tip of the cue, then throwing up another and catching that on top of the first ball—which he often missed. For four years, he told Mr Jackson, he had been practising that trick and at the end of the week he intended to try it out for the first time with the audience. That night we all stood in the wings and watched him. He did it perfectly, and the first time!—throwing the ball up and catching it on the tip of the billiard cue, then throwing a second and catching that on top of the first. But the audience only applauded mildly. Mr Jackson often told the story of that night. Said he to Zarmo: 'You make the trick look too easy, you don't sell it. You should miss it several times, then do it.' Zarmo laughed. 'I am not expert enough to miss it yet.' Zarmo was also interested in phrenology and would read our characters. He told me that whatever knowledge I acquired, I would retain and put to good use.

And there were the Griffiths Brothers, funny and impressive, who confused my psychology, comedy trapeze clowns who, as they both swung from the trapeze, would ferociously kick each other in the face with large padded shoes.

'Ouch!' said the receiver. 'I dare you to do it again!'

'Do yer?' ... Bang!

And the receiver would look surprised and groggy and say: 'He did it again!'

I thought such crazy violence shocking. But off stage they were devoted brothers, quiet and serious.

Dan Leno, I suppose, was the greatest English comedian since the legendary Grimaldi. Although I never saw Leno in his prime, to me he was more of a character actor than a comedian. His whimsical character delineations of London's lower classes were human and endearing, so Mother told me.

The famous Marie Lloyd was reputed to be frivolous, yet when we played with her at the old Tivoli in the Strand never was there a more serious and conscientious artist. I would watch her wide-eyed, this anxious, plump little lady pacing nervously up and down behind the scenes, irritable and apprehensive until the moment came for her to go on. Then she was immediately gay and relaxed.

And Bransby Williams, the Dickens delineator, enthralled me with imitations of Uriah Heep, Bill Sykes and the old man of *The Old Curiosity Shop*. The legerdemain of this handsome, dignified young man making up before a rowdy Glasgow audience and transforming himself into these fascinating characters, opened up another aspect of the theatre. He also ignited my curiosity about literature; I wanted to know what was this immured mystery that lay hidden in books—these sepia Dickens characters that moved in such a strange Cruikshankian world. Although I could hardly read, I eventually bought *Oliver Twist*.

43

So enthralled was I with Dickens characters that I would imitate Bransby Williams imitating them. It was inevitable that such budding talent could not be concealed for long. Thus it was that one day Mr Jackson saw me entertaining the other boys with an imitation of the old man of *The Old Curiosity Shop*. Then and there I was proclaimed a genius, and Mr Jackson was determined to let the world know it.

The momentous event happened at the theatre in Middlesbrough. After our clog dance Mr Jackson walked on stage with the earnestness of one about to announce the coming of a young Messiah, stating that he had discovered a child genius among his boys, who would give an imitation of Bransby Williams as the old man of *The Old Curiosity Shop* who cannot recognise the death of his little Nell.

The audience were not too receptive, having endured a very boring evening's entertainment already. However, I came on wearing my usual dancing costume of a white linen blouse, a lace collar, plush knickerbocker pants and red dancing shoes, and made up to look like an old man of ninety. Somewhere, somehow, we had come into possession of an old wig—Mr Jackson might have bought it—but it did not fit me. Although I had a large head, the wig was larger; it was a bald-headed wig fringed with long, grey, stringy hair, so that when I appeared on the stage bent as an old man, the effect was like a crawling beetle, and the audience endorsed the fact with their titters.

It was difficult to get them quiet after that. I spoke in subdued whispers: 'Hush, hush, you mustn't make a noise or you'll wake my Nelly.'

'Louder! Louder! Speak up!' shouted the audience.

But I went on feebly whispering, all very intimate; so intimate that the audience began to stamp. It was the end of my career as a delineator of Charles Dickens' characters.

Although we lived frugally, life with the Eight Lancashire Lads was agreeable. Occasionally we had our little dissensions. I remember playing on the same bill with two young acrobats, boy apprentices about my own age, who told us confidentially that their mothers received seven and sixpence a week and they got a shilling pocket money put under their bacon-and-egg plate every Monday morning. 'And,' complained one of our boys, 'we only get twopence and a bread and jam breakfast.'

When Mr Jackson's son, John, heard that we were complaining, he broke down and wept, telling us that at times, playing odd weeks in the suburbs of London, his father only got seven pounds a week for the whole troupe and that they were having a hard time making both ends meet.

It was this opulent living of the two young apprentices that made us ambitious to become acrobats. So for several mornings, as soon as the theatre opened, one or two of us would practise somersaults with a rope tied round our waists, attached to a pulley, while one of us would hold the rope. I did very well turning somersaults in this fashion until I fell and sprained my thumb. That ended my acrobatic career.

Besides dancing we were always trying to add to our other accomplishments. I wanted to be a comedy juggler, so I had saved enough money to buy four rubber balls and four tin plates and for hours I would stand over the bedside, practising.

Mr Jackson was essentially a good man. Three months before I left the troupe we appeared at a benefit for my father, who had been very ill; many vaudeville artists donated their services, including Mr Jackson's Eight Lancashire Lads. The night of the benefit my father appeared on the stage breathing with difficulty, and with painful effort made a speech. I stood at the side of the stage watching him, not realising that he was a dying man.

When we were in London, I visited Mother every week-end. She thought I looked pale and thin and that dancing was affecting my lungs. It worried her so much that she wrote about it to Mr Jackson, who was so indignant that he finally sent me home, saying that I was not worth the bother of such a worrying mother.

A few weeks later, however, I developed asthma. The attacks grew so severe that Mother was convinced I had tuberculosis and promptly took me to Brompton Hospital, where I was given a thorough examination. Nothing was found wrong with my lungs, but I did have asthma. For months I went through agony, unable to breathe. At times I wanted to jump out of the window. Inhaling herbs with a blanket over my head gave little relief. But, as the doctor said I would, I eventually outgrew it.

My memory of this period goes in and out of focus. The outstanding impression was a quagmire of miserable circumstances. I cannot remember where Sydney was; being four years older, he only occasionally entered my consciousness. He was possibly living with Grandfather to relieve Mother's penury. We seemed to vacillate from one abode to another, eventually ending up in a small garret at 3 Pownall Terrace.

I was well aware of the social stigma of our poverty. Even the poorest of children sat down to a home-cooked Sunday dinner. A roast at home meant respectability, a ritual that distinguished one poor class from another. Those who could not sit down to Sunday dinner at home were of the mendicant class, and we were that. Mother would send me to the nearest coffee-shop to buy a sixpenny dinner (meat and two vegetables). The shame of it—especially on Sunday! I would harry her for not preparing something at home, and she would vainly try to explain that cooking at home would cost twice as much.

However, one lucky Friday, after winning five shillings at horse-racing, Mother, to please me, decided to cook dinner on Sunday. Amongst other delectables she bought a piece of roasting meat that could not make up its mind whether to be beef or a lump of suet. It weighed about five pounds and had a sign stuck in it: 'For Roasting'.

Mother, having no oven, used the landlady's and, being too shy to keep going in and out of her kitchen, had haphazardly guessed the time needed to roast it. Consequently, to our dismay, our joint had shrunk to the size of a cricket ball.

Nevertheless, in spite of Mother's averring that our sixpenny dinners were less trouble and more palatable, I enjoyed it and felt the gratification of having lived up to the Joneses.

*   *   *

A sudden change came into our lives. Mother met an old friend who had become very prosperous, a flamboyant, good-looking, Junoesque type of woman who had given up the stage to become the mistress of a wealthy old colonel. She lived in the fashionable district of Stockwell; and in her enthusiasm at meeting Mother again, she invited us to stay with her during the summer. As Sydney was away in the country hop-picking, it took little inducement to persuade Mother, who, with the wizardry of her needle made herself quite presentable, and I, dressed in my Sunday suit, a relic of the Eight Lancashire Lads, looked quite presentable for the occasion.

Thus overnight we were transported to a very sedate corner house in Lansdowne Square, ensconced in the lap of luxury, with a house full of servants, pink and blue bedrooms, chintz curtains and white bear-rugs; moreover, we lived on the fat of the land. How well I remember those large, blue, hothouse grapes that ornamented the sideboard in the dining-room and my feeling of guilt at their mysterious diminishing, looking more skeleton-like each day.

The household staff consisted of four women: the cook and three maids. In addition to Mother and me, there was another guest, a very tense, good-looking young man with a cropped red moustache. He was most charming and gentlemanly, and seemed a permanent fixture in the house—until the grey-whiskered Colonel appeared. Then the handsome young man would disappear.

The Colonel's visits were sporadic, once or twice a week. While he was there, mystery and omnipresence pervaded the house, and Mother would tell me to keep out of the way and not to be seen. One day I ran into the hall as the Colonel was

47

descending the stairs. He was a tall, stately gentleman in a frock-coat and top hat, a pink face, long grey side-burns and a bald head. He smiled benignly at me and went on his way.

I did not understand what all the hush and fuss was about and why the Colonel's arrival created such an effect. But he never stayed long, and the young man with the cropped moustache would return, and the house would function normally again.

I grew very fond of the young man with the cropped moustache. We would take long walks together over Clapham Common with the lady's two beautiful greyhound dogs. Clapham Common had an elegant atmosphere in those days. Even the chemist's shop, where we occasionally made a purchase, exuded elegance with its familiar admixture of aromatic smells, perfumes, soaps and powders—ever since, the odour of certain chemists' shops has a pleasant nostalgia. He advised Mother to have me take cold baths every morning to cure my asthma, and possibly they helped; they were most invigorating and I grew to like them.

It is remarkable how easily one adapts oneself to the social graces. How genteel and accustomed one becomes to creature comforts! In less than a week I took everything for granted. What a sense of well-being—going through that morning ritual, exercising the dogs, carrying their new brown leather leashes, then returning to a beautiful house with servants, to await lunch served in elegant style on silver platters.

Our back garden connected with another house whose occupants had as many servants as we had. They were a family of three, a young married couple and their son, who was about my own age and who had a nursery stocked with beautiful toys. I was often invited to play with him and to stay for dinner, and we became very good friends. His father held some important position in a City bank, and his mother was young and quite pretty.

One day I overheard our maid confidentially conversing with

4. My father

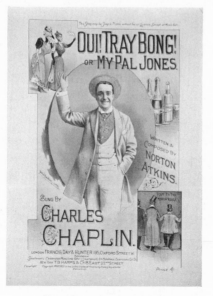

5. He too was a vaudevillian,
with an excellent light baritone voice

6. The garret, the top two windows, at 3 Pownall Terrace, Kennington Road

7. The first floor of 287 Kennington Road, where Sydney and I lived with Louise and Father

8. Where we lived, next to the slaughter-house and the pickle factory, after Mother came out of the asylum

9. Lambeth Workhouse

the boy's maid, who was saying that their boy needed a gover-
ness. 'That's what this one needs,' said our maid, referring to
me. I was thrilled to be looked upon as a child of the rich, but
I never quite understood why she had elevated me to this status,
unless it was to elevate herself by inferring that the people she
worked for were as well off and as respectable as the neighbours
next door. After that, whenever I dined with the boy next door
I felt somewhat of an impostor.

Although it was a mournful day when we left the fine house
to return to 3 Pownall Terrace, yet there was a sense of relief
in getting back to our own freedom; after all, as guests we were
living under a certain tension, and, as Mother said, guests
were like cakes: if kept too long they became stale and un-
palatable. Thus the silken threads of a brief and luxurious
episode snapped, and we fell again into our accustomed im-
pecunious ways.

IV

1899 was an epoch of whiskers: bewhiskered kings, statesmen, soldiers and sailors, Krugers, Salisburys, Kitcheners, Kaisers and cricketers—incredible years of pomp and absurdity, of extreme wealth and poverty, of inane political bigotry of both cartoon and press. But England was to absorb many shocks and indignations. A few Boer farmers in the African Transvaal were warring unfairly, shooting our red-coated soldiers, excellent targets, from behind boulders and rocks. Then the War Office saw the light, and our red coats were quickly changed to khaki. If the Boers wanted it that way, they could have it.

I was vaguely aware of war through patriotic songs, vaudeville sketches and cigarette pictures of the generals. The enemy, of course, were unmitigated villains. One heard dolorous news about the Boers surrounding Ladysmith and England went mad with hysterical joy at the relief of Mafeking. Then at last we won —we muddled through. All this I heard from everyone but Mother. She never mentioned the war. She had her own battle to fight.

Sydney was now fourteen and had left school and got a job at the Strand Post Office as a telegraph boy. With Sydney's wages and Mother's earnings at her sewing machine, our economy was almost feasible—although Mother's contribution was a modest one. She worked for a sweat-shop doing piece-work, sewing blouses for one and sixpence a dozen. Even though the patterns were delivered already cut out, it took twelve hours to make a dozen blouses. Mother's record was fifty-four blouses in a week, which amounted to six shillings and ninepence.

Often at night I would lie awake in our garret watching her bent over her sewing machine, her head haloed against the light of the oil-lamp, her face in soft shadow, her lips faintly parted with strain as she guided the rapidly running seams through her machine, until the drone of it would send me off to sleep again. When she worked late this way, it was usually to meet a monetary deadline. There was always the problem of instalment payments.

And now a crisis had arisen. Sydney needed a new suit of clothes. He had worn his telegraph uniform every day in the week, including Sundays, until his friends began to joke about it. So for a couple of week-ends he stayed home until Mother was able to buy him a blue serge suit. In some way she managed to scrape together eighteen shillings. This created an insolvency in our economy, so that Mother was obliged to pawn the suit every Monday after Sydney went back to work in his telegraph uniform. She got seven shillings for the suit, redeeming it every Saturday for Sydney to wear over the week-end. This weekly custom became an habitual ceremony for over a year until the suit became threadbare. Then came a shock!

Monday morning, as usual, Mother went to the pawnshop. The man hesitated. 'I'm sorry, Mrs Chaplin, but we can't lend you seven shillings any longer.'

Mother was astonished. 'But why?' she asked.

'It's too much of a risk; the trousers are threadbare. Look,' he said, putting his hand in the seat of them, 'you can see right through them.'

'But they'll be redeemed next Saturday,' said Mother.

The pawnbroker shook his head. 'The best I can do is three shillings for the coat and waistcoat.'

Mother rarely wept, but it was such a drastic blow that she came home in tears. She depended on that seven shillings to carry us through the week.

Meanwhile my own vestments were, to say the least, in disrepair. What was left of my Eight Lancashire Lads' outfit was a motley sight. There were patches everywhere, on the elbows, trousers, shoes and stockings. And in this condition I ran smack into my nice little boy friend from Stockwell. What he was doing in Kennington I did not know and was too embarrassed to find out. He greeted me friendlily enough, but

51

I could see him eyeing my deplorable appearance. To offset my embarrassment I assumed a *dégagé* manner and in my best, cultured voice told him that I was wearing my old clothes because I had just come from a beastly carpentry lesson.

But the explanation had little interest for him. He began to look crestfallen and to cast his eyes aside to hide his embarrassment. He enquired after Mother.

I answered briskly that she was away in the country and turned the attention on him: 'Are you living in the same place?'

'Yes,' he answered, surveying me as though I had committed some cardinal sin.

'Well, I'll run along,' I said abruptly.

He faintly smiled. 'Goodbye,' he said, and we parted, he walking off sedately in one direction and I, furious and ashamed, running helter-skelter in the opposite one.

*   *   *

Mother had a saying: 'You can always stoop and pick up nothing.' But she herself did not adhere to this adage, and my sense of propriety was often outraged. One day, returning from Brompton Hospital, Mother stopped to upbraid some boys tormenting a derelict woman who was grotesquely ragged and dirty. She had a cropped head, unusual in those days, and the boys were laughing and pushing each other towards her, as if to touch her would contaminate them. The pathetic woman stood like a stag at bay until Mother interfered. Then a look of recognition came over the woman's face. 'Lil,' she said, feebly, referring to Mother's stage name, 'don't you know me—Eva Lestock?'

Mother recognised her at once, an old friend of her vaudeville days.

I was so embarrassed that I moved on and waited for Mother at the corner. The boys walked past me, smirking and giggling. I was furious. I turned to see what was happening to Mother and, lo, the derelict woman had joined her and both were walking towards me.

Said Mother: 'You remember little Charlie?'

'Do I!' said the woman, dolefully. 'I've held him in my arms many a time when he was a baby.'

The thought was repellent, for the woman looked so filthy and loathsome. And as we walked along, it was embarrassing to see people turn and look at the three of us.

Mother had known her in vaudeville as 'the Dashing Eva Lestock'; she was pretty and vivacious then, so Mother told me. The woman said that she had been ill in the hospital, and that since leaving it, she had been sleeping under arches and in Salvation Army shelters.

First Mother sent her to the public baths, then to my horror brought her home to our small garret. Whether it was illness alone that was the cause of her present circumstances, I never knew. What was outrageous was that she slept in Sydney's armchair bed. However, Mother gave her what clothes she could spare and loaned her a couple of bob. After three days she departed, and that was the last we ever saw or heard of 'the Dashing Eva Lestock'!

*　　　*　　　*

Before Father died, Mother moved from Pownall Terrace and rented a room at the house of Mrs Taylor, a friend of Mother's, a church member and devoted Christian. She was a short, square-framed woman in her middle fifties with a square jaw and a sallow, wrinkled face. While watching her in church I discovered she had false teeth. They would drop from her upper gums on to her tongue while she sang—the effect was hypnotic.

She had an emphatic manner and abundant energy. She had taken Mother under her Christian wing, and had rented her a front room, at a very reasonable rent, on the second floor of her large house which was next to a graveyard.

Her husband, a facsimile of Dickens' Mr Pickwick, was a precision ruler maker and had his workshop on the top floor. The roof had a skylight and I thought the place heavenly, it was so peaceful there. I often watched Mr Taylor at work, fascinated as he peered intensely through his thick-lensed spectacles with a large magnifying glass, making a steel ruler that would measure one-fiftieth part of an inch. He worked alone and I often ran errands for him.

Mrs Taylor's one desire was to convert her husband, who, according to her Christian scruples, was a sinner. Her daughter, whose features were of the same cast as the mother's except that she was less sallow and, of course, much younger, would have been attractive but for her hauteur and objectionable manner. Like her father, she never attended church. But Mrs Taylor never gave up hope of converting them both. The daughter was the apple of her mother's eye—but not of my mother's eye.

One afternoon, while on the top floor watching Mr Taylor at work, I heard an altercation below between Mother and Miss Taylor. Mrs Taylor was out. I do not know how it started, but they were both shouting loudly at each other. As I reached our landing, Mother was leaning over the banisters: 'Who do you think you are? Lady Shit?'

'Oh!' shouted the daughter. 'That's nice language coming from a Christian!'

'Don't worry,' said Mother quickly, 'it's in the Bible, my dear: Deuteronomy, twenty-eighth chapter, thirty-seventh verse, only there's another word for it. However, shit will suit you.'

After that, we moved back to Pownall Terrace.

*　　　*　　　*

The Three Stags in the Kennington Road was not a place my father frequented, yet as I passed it one evening an urge prompted me to peek inside to see if he was there. I opened the saloon door just a few inches, and there he was, sitting in the corner! I was about to leave, but his face lit up and he beckoned me to him. I was surprised at such a welcome, for he was never demonstrative. He looked very ill; his eyes were sunken, and his body had swollen to an enormous size. He rested one hand, Napoleon-like, in his waistcoat as if to ease his difficult breathing. That evening he was most solicitous, enquiring after Mother and Sydney, and before I left took me in his arms and for the first time kissed me. That was the last time I saw him alive.

Three weeks later, he was taken to St Thomas's Hospital. They had to get him drunk to get him there. When he realised where he was, he fought wildly—but he was a dying man. Though still very young, only thirty-seven, he was dying of dropsy. They tapped sixteen quarts of liquid from his knee.

Mother went several times to see him and was always saddened by the visit. She said he spoke of wanting to go back to her and start life anew in Africa. When I brightened at such a prospect, Mother shook her head, for she knew better. 'He was saying that only to be nice,' she said.

One day she came home from the hospital indignant over what the Reverend John McNeil, Evangelist, had said when he paid Father a visit: 'Well, Charlie, when I look at you, I can only think of the old proverb: "Whatsoever a man soweth, that shall he also reap".'

'Nice words to console a dying man,' said Mother. A few days later Father was dead.

The hospital wanted to know who would bury him. Mother, not having a penny, suggested the Variety Artists' Benevolent Fund, a theatrical charity organisation. This caused an uproar with the Chaplin side of the family—the humiliation of being buried by charity was repugnant to them. An Uncle Albert from Africa, my father's youngest brother, was in London at the time and said he would pay for the burial.

The day of the funeral we were to meet at St Thomas's Hospital, where we were to join the rest of the Chaplins and from there drive out to Tooting Cemetery. Sydney could not come, as he was working. Mother and I arrived at the hospital a couple of hours before the allotted time because she wanted to see Father before he was enclosed.

The coffin was enshrouded in white satin and around the edge of it, framing Father's face, were little white daisies. Mother thought they looked so simple and touching and asked who had placed them there. The attendant told her that a lady had called early that morning with a little boy. It was Louise.

In the first carriage were Mother, Uncle Albert and me. The drive to Tooting was a strain, for she had never met Uncle Albert before. He was somewhat of a dandy and spoke with a cultured accent; although polite, his attitude was icy. He was reputed to be rich; he had large horse ranches in the Transvaal and had provided the British Government with horses during the Boer War.

It poured with rain during the service; the grave-diggers threw down clods of earth on the coffin which resounded with a brutal thud. It was macabre and horrifying and I began to weep. Then the relatives threw in their wreaths and flowers. Mother, having nothing to throw in, took my precious black-bordered handkerchief. 'Here, sonny,' she whispered, 'this will do for both of us.' Afterwards the Chaplins stopped off at one of their pubs for lunch, and before leaving asked us politely where we desired to be dropped. So we were driven home.

When we returned there was not a particle of food in the cupboard except a saucer of beef dripping, and Mother had not a penny, for she had given Sydney her last twopence for his lunch money. Since Father's illness she had done little work, and now, near the end of the week, Sydney's wages of seven shillings as a telegraph boy had already run out. After the funeral we were hungry. Luckily the rag-and-bone man was passing outside and we had an old oil stove, so reluctantly she sold it for a halfpenny and bought a halfpenny worth of bread to go with the dripping.

Mother, being the legal widow of my father, was told the

next day to call at the hospital for his belongings, which consisted of a black suit spotted with blood, underwear, a shirt, a black tie, an old dressing-gown, and some plaid house slippers with oranges stuffed in the toes. When she took the oranges out, a half sovereign fell out of the slippers on to the bed. This was a godsend!

For weeks I wore crêpe on my arm. These insignia of grief became profitable when I went into business on a Saturday afternoon, selling flowers. I had persuaded Mother to loan me a shilling, and went to the flower market and purchased two bundles of narcissus, and after school busied myself making them into penny bundles. All sold, I could make a hundred per cent profit.

I would go into the saloons, looking wistful, and whisper: 'Narcissus, miss!' 'Narcissus, madame!' The women always responded: 'Who is it, son?' And I would lower my voice to a whisper: 'My father,' and they would give me tips. Mother was amazed when I came home in the evening with more than five shillings for an afternoon's work. One day she bumped into me as I came out of a pub, and that put an end to my flower-selling; that her boy was peddling flowers in bar-rooms offended her Christian scruples. 'Drink killed your father, and money from such a source will only bring us bad luck,' she said. However, she kept the proceeds, though she never allowed me to sell flowers again.

There was a strong element of the merchant in me. I was continuously preoccupied with business schemes. I would look at empty shops, speculating as to what profitable businesses I could make of them, ranging from fish and chips to grocery shops. It had always to do with food. All I needed was capital—but how does one get capital? Eventually I talked Mother into letting me leave school and get a job.

I became a veteran of many occupations. First I was an errand boy in a chandler's shop. Between errands I was delightfully occupied in the cellar, immured in soap, starch, candles, sweets and biscuits, sampling all the sweetmeats till I made myself sick.

Then I was a doctor's boy for Hool and Kinsey-Taylor, insurance doctors in Throgmorton Avenue, a job I inherited from Sydney, who recommended me. It was lucrative, and I was paid twelve shillings a week to act as receptionist with the duties of cleaning out the offices after the doctors had gone. As a receptionist I was a great success and charmed all the waiting patients, but when it came to cleaning up the offices my heart was not in it—Sydney was much better. I did not mind emptying the phials of urine, but cleaning those ten-foot office windows was indeed a gargantuan task; so that the offices grew dimmer and dustier until I was told politely that I was too small for the job.

When I heard the news I broke down and wept. Dr Kinsey-Taylor, married to a very wealthy lady with a large house in Lancaster Gate, took pity on me and said he would fit me in as a page-boy in his house. Immediately my heart lightened. A page-boy in a private house, and a very posh one at that!

It was a happy job, for I was the pet of all the housemaids. They treated me like a child and kissed me good-night before I went to bed. But for Fate I might have become a butler. Madame wanted me to clean out a cellar in the area where there were packing cases and debris piled high that had to be sorted, cleaned and arranged. I was diverted from the task by my interest in an iron pipe about eight feet long, through which I blew like a trumpet. Just as I was enjoying myself, Madame appeared—and I was given three days' notice.

I enjoyed working for W. H. Smith and Son, the stationers, but lost the job as soon as they found I was under age. Then for a day I was a glass-blower. I had read about glass-blowing at school and thought it romantic, but the heat overcame me and I was carried out unconscious and laid on a sand pile. That was enough; I never went back even to collect my day's salary. Then I worked at Straker's, the printers and stationers. I tried to bluff them that I could run a Wharfedale printing machine—an enormous thing, over twenty feet long. I had seen it in action, looking into the cellar from the street, and the task looked easy and simple to do. A card read: 'Boy wanted as layer-on for a Wharfedale printing machine.' When the foreman brought me to it, it loomed up monstrously. To operate it, I had to stand upon a platform five feet high. I felt I was at the top of the Eiffel Tower.

'Strike her!' said the foreman.

'Strike her?'

Seeing me hesitate, he laughed. 'You've never worked on a Wharfedale.'

'Just give me the chance, I'll pick it up quite easily,' I said.

'Strike her' meant pull the lever to start the brute. He showed me the lever, then put the beast at half-speed. It started to roll, grind and grunt; I thought it was going to devour me. The sheets were enormous; you could have wrapped me in one. With an ivory scraper I fanned the paper sheets, picking them up by the corners and placing them meticulously against the teeth in time for the monster to clutch them, devour them and regurgitate until they rolled out at the rear end. The first day I was a nervous wreck from the hungry brute wanting to get ahead of me. Nevertheless, I was given the job at twelve shillings per week.

There was romance and adventure about getting out on those cold mornings, before daylight, and going to work, the streets silent and deserted except for one or two shadowy figures making their way to the beacon light of Lockhart's tea-room for breakfast. One had a feeling of well-being with one's fellow men, sipping hot tea in the glow and warmth of that momentary respite before a day's work. And the printing job was not unpleasant; but for the heavy work at the end of the week, having to wash the ink off those tall, heavy, gelatine rollers weighing more than a hundred pounds each, the work was tolerable. However, after three weeks there, I came down with influenza, and Mother insisted that I return to school.

Sydney was now sixteen, and came home excited because he had obtained a job as a bugler on a Donovan and Castle Line passenger boat sailing to Africa. His duties were to blow the calls for lunch etc. He had learnt to play the bugle on the *Exmouth* training ship; now it was paying off. He was to receive two pounds ten a month, and tips from waiting at three tables in the second class. Thirty-five shillings he was to get in advance before sailing, which, of course, he would give to Mother. With such happy prospect, we moved into two rooms over a barber's shop in Chester Street.

Sydney's return from his first trip was the occasion for celebration, for he came back with over three pounds in tips and all in silver. I remember him pouring the money out of his pockets on to the bed. It seemed more money than I had ever seen in my life and I could not keep my hands off it. I scooped it up, dropped it, stacked it and played with it until both Mother and Sydney declared that I was a miser.

What luxury! What indulgence! It was summer and this was our cake and ice-cream period—we had many other luxuries besides. It was also our period of bloaters, kippers, haddocks and toasted tea-cakes for breakfast, and muffins and crumpets on Sunday morning.

Sydney caught cold and languished in bed for several days, and Mother and I waited on him. It was then that we indulged ourselves in ice-cream, a pennyworth in a large tumbler which I presented at the Italian ice-cream shop, much to the irritation of the owner. On my second visit he suggested I bring a bath-tub. A favourite summer drink of ours was sherbet and milk—the sherbet fizzing up through the over-skimmed milk was indeed delectable.

Sydney told us many amusing stories about his voyage. Before sailing he almost lost the job when he blew the first bugle call for lunch. He was out of practice and the soldiers aboard let up a chorus of howls. The chief steward came in a fury. 'What the hell do you call that?' 'Sorry, sir,' said Sydney, 'I haven't got my lip in yet.' 'Well, you'd better get your bloody lip in before the boat sails, otherwise you'll be put ashore.'

During meals there would be a long line of stewards in the kitchen filling their orders. But by the time Sydney's turn came he had forgotten his order, so he would have to go to the end of the line again. Sydney said that for the first few days while everyone was finishing their dessert he was serving soup.

Sydney stayed home until his money was spent. However, he was booked for a second trip and again they advanced him thirty-five shillings, which he gave to Mother. But this did not last long. After three weeks we were scraping the bottom of the barrel, and there was another three weeks to go before Sydney's return. Although Mother continued working at her sewing machine, what she earned was not enough to keep us going. Consequently we were in another crisis.

But I was resourceful. Mother had a pile of old clothes, and, as it was Saturday morning, I suggested that I should try and sell them in the market place. Mother was a little embarrassed, and said they were quite worthless. Nevertheless, I wrapped them up in an old sheet and wended my way to Newington Butts and there laid my ignoble congeries on the pavement—a drab and sorry sight—then stood in the gutter and shouted: 'Here!' —picking up an old shirt, then a pair of old corsets—'what will you give me?—a shilling, sixpence, threepence, twopence?' Not even at a penny could I make a sale. People would stop, look astonished, then laugh and go on their way. I began to feel embarrassed, especially when the occupants of a jeweller's shop opposite began looking at me through the shop window. However, nothing deterred me. Eventually a pair of gaiters that did not look so depressing sold for sixpence. But the longer I stayed the uneasier I felt. Later the gentleman from the jeweller's shop came over to me and asked, in a thick Russian accent, how long I had been in business. In spite of his solemn face, I detected humour in his remark and told him I had just started. He walked slowly back to his two grinning partners, who were looking through the shop window at me. That was enough! I thought it time to wrap up my wares and return home. When I told Mother I had sold a pair of gaiters for sixpence, she was indignant. 'They should have brought more,' she said. 'They were a beautiful pair!'

At this juncture we were not too concerned about paying rent; that problem was easily solved by being out for the day when the rent man called, and, as our belongings were of little value, it would cost more than we owed to cart them away. However, we moved back to 3 Pownall Terrace.

At this time I came to know an old man and his son who worked in a mews at the back of Kennington Road. They were travelling toy-makers who came from Glasgow, making toys and selling them as they wandered from town to town. They were free and unencumbered and I envied them. Their profession needed little capital. With as small an investment as a shilling they could start in business. They would collect shoe-boxes, which every shoe-shop was only too pleased to give them, and cork sawdust in which grapes were packed which they also got gratis. Their initial outlay consisted only in the purchase of a pennyworth of glue, a pennyworth of wood, twopence worth of twine, a pennyworth of Christmas coloured paper and three twopenny balls of coloured tinsel. For a shilling they could make seven dozen boats and sell them for a penny apiece. The sides were cut from shoe-boxes and were sewn on to a cardboard base, the smooth surface was covered with glue, then poured over with cork sawdust. The masts were rigged with coloured tinsel, and blue, yellow and red flags were stuck on the topmast and on the end of the booms, fore and aft. A hundred or more of these little toy boats, with their coloured tinsel and flags, was a gay and festive sight that attracted customers, and they were easy to sell.

As a result of our acquaintance I began helping them to make boats, and very soon I was familiar with their craft. When they left our neighbourhood I went into business for myself. With a limited capital of sixpence, and at the cost of blistered hands through cutting up cardboard, I was able to turn out three dozen boats within a week.

But there was not enough space in our garret for Mother's work and my boat-making. Besides, Mother complained of the odour of boiling glue, and that the glue pot was a constant menace to her linen blouses, which, incidentally, crowded most of the space in the room. As my contribution was less than Mother's, her work took precedence and my craft was abandoned.

We had seen little of Grandfather during this time. For the past year he had not been doing too well. His hands were swollen with gout, which made it difficult for him to work at his shoe-repairing. In the past he had helped Mother when he could afford with a couple of bob or so. Sometimes he would cook dinner for us, a wonderful bargoo stew composed of Quaker Oats and onions boiled in milk with salt and pepper. On a wintry night it was our constitutional base to withstand the cold.

As a boy I thought Grandpa a dour, fractious old man who was always correcting me either about my manners or my grammar. Because of these small encounters, I had grown to dislike him. Now he was in the infirmary with rheumatism, and Mother would go every visiting day to see him. These visits were profitable, because she usually returned with a bag full of fresh eggs, quite a luxury in our recessional period. When unable to go herself, she would send me. I was always surprised when I found Grandpa most agreeable and happy to see me. He was quite a favourite with the nurses. He told me in later life that he would joke with them, saying that in spite of his crippling rheumatism not all his machinery was impaired. This sort of rodomontade amused the nurses. When his rheumatism allowed him, he worked in the kitchen, whence came our eggs. On visiting days, he was usually in bed, and from his bedside cabinet would surreptitiously hand me a large bag of them, which I quickly stowed in my sailor's tunic before departing.

For weeks we lived on eggs, dished up in every form, boiled, fried and custardised. In spite of Grandpa's assurance that the nurses were his friends and knew more or less what was going on, I was always apprehensive when leaving the hospital ward with those eggs, terrified of slipping on the beeswax polished floor, or that my tumorous bulk would be apprehended. Curiously enough, when I was ready to leave, the nurses were always conspicuous by their absence. It was a sorry day for us when Grandpa was rid of his rheumatism and left the hospital.

Now six weeks had elapsed and still Sydney had not returned. At first this did not alarm Mother, but after several week's delay she wrote to the offices of the Donovan and Castle Line and received information that he had been put ashore at Cape Town for treatment of rheumatic fever, which worried Mother and affected her health. Still she continued working on her sewing machine and I was fortunate in obtaining a little work by giving a few dancing lessons to a family after school for the sum of five shillings a week.

About this time the McCarthys came to live in Kennington Road. Mrs McCarthy had been an Irish comedienne and was a friend of Mother's. She was married to Walter McCarthy, a chartered accountant. But when Mother was obliged to give up the stage we lost sight of Mr and Mrs McCarthy and not until seven years later did we meet them again, when they came to live at Walcott Mansions in the select part of Kennington Road.

Their son, Wally McCarthy, and I were the same age. As little children, we used to play at grown-ups, pretending we were vaudevillians, smoking our imaginary cigars and driving in our imaginary pony and trap, much to the amusement of our parents.

Since the McCarthys had come to live in Walcott Mansions, Mother had rarely seen them, but Wally and I had formed an inseparable friendship. As soon as I was through with school I would race home to Mother to find out if she needed any errands done, then race up to the McCarthys'. We would play theatre at the back of Walcott Mansions. As the director, I always gave myself the villain parts, knowing instinctively they were more colourful than the hero. We would play until Wally's supper-time. Usually I was invited. At mealtimes I had an ingratiating way of making myself available. There were occasions, however, when my manœuvring did not work and I would reluctantly return home. Mother was always happy to see me and would prepare something for me, fried bread in dripping or one of Grandfather's eggs and a cup of tea. She would read to me or we would sit together at the window and she would amuse me by making remarks about the pedestrians as they passed by. She would invent stories about them. If it were a young man with a breezy, bobbing gait she would say: 'There goes Mr Hopandscotch. He's on his way to place a bet. If he's lucky today he's going to buy a second-hand tandem for him and his girl.'

Then a man would pass slowly, moping along. 'Hm, he's going home to have stew and parsnips for dinner, which he hates.'

Then someone with an air of superiority would walk by. 'Now there's a refined young man, but at the moment he's worried about the hole in the seat of his pants.'

Then another with a fast gait would streak past. 'That gentleman has just taken Eno's!' And so she would go on, send-ing me into gales of laughter.

Another week had gone by and not a word from Sydney. Had I been less a boy and more sensitive to Mother's anxiety I might have realised what was impending. I might have noticed that for several days she had been sitting listlessly at the window, had neglected to tidy up the room, had grown unusu-ally quiet. I might have been concerned when the firm of shirtmakers began finding fault with her work and stopped giving it to her, and when they took away her sewing machine for arrears in payments, and when the five shillings I earned from dancing lessons suddenly ended; through all this I might have noticed that Mother remained indifferent, apathetic.

Mrs McCarthy suddenly died. She had been ailing for some time, and her health rapidly deteriorated until she passed on. Immediately, thoughts invaded my mind: how wonderful if Mr McCarthy married Mother—Wally and I being such good friends. Besides, it would be an ideal solution to all Mother's problems.

Soon after the funeral I spoke to Mother about it: 'You should make it your business to see a lot of Mr McCarthy. I bet he'd like to marry you.'

Mother smiled wanly. 'Give the poor man a chance,' she said.

'If you were all dressed up and made yourself attractive, as you used to be, he would. But you don't make any effort; all you do is to sit around this filthy room and look awful.'

Poor Mother. How I regret those words. I never realised that she was weak from malnutrition. Yet the next day, by some superhuman effort, she had tidied up the room.

The school's summer holidays were on, so I thought I would go early to the McCarthys'—anything to get away from the wretchedness of our garret. They had invited me to stay for lunch, but I had an intuition that I should return home to Mother. When I reached Pownall Terrace, I was stopped at the gate by some children of the neighbourhood.

'Your mother's gone insane,' said a little girl.

The words were like a slap in the face.

'What do you mean?' I mumbled.

'It's true,' said another. 'She's been knocking at all our doors, giving away pieces of coal, saying they were birthday presents for the children. You can ask my mother.'

Without hearing more, I ran up the pathway, through the open door of the house and leaped up the stairs and opened the door of our room. I stood a moment to catch my breath, intensely scrutinising her. It was a summer's afternoon and the atmosphere was close and oppressive. Mother was sitting as usual at the window. She turned slowly and looked at me, her face pale and tormented.

'Mother!' I almost shouted.

'What is it?' she said listlessly.

Then I ran and fell on my knees and buried my face in her lap, and burst into uncontrollable weeping.

'There, there,' she said gently, stroking my head. 'What's wrong?'

'You're not well,' I cried between sobs.

She spoke reassuringly: 'Of course I am.'

She seemed so vague, so preoccupied.

'No! No! They say you've been going to all the houses and—' I could not finish, but continued sobbing.

'I was looking for Sydney,' she said weakly; 'they're keeping him away from me.'

Then I knew that what the children had said was true.

'Oh, Mummy, don't talk like that! Don't! Don't!' I sobbed. 'Let me get you a doctor.'

She continued, stroking my head: 'The McCarthys know where he is, and they're keeping him away from me.'

'Mummy, please let me get a doctor,' I cried. I got up and went towards the door.

She looked after me with a pained expression. 'Where are you going?'

'To get a doctor. I won't be long.'

She never answered, but looked anxiously after me. Quickly I rushed downstairs to the landlady. 'I've got to get a doctor at once, Mother's not well!'

'We've already sent for him,' the landlady said.

The parish doctor was old and grumpy and after hearing the landlady's story, which was similar to that of the children, he made a perfunctory examination of Mother. 'Insane. Send her to the infirmary,' he said.

The doctor wrote out a paper; besides other things it said she

67

was suffering from malnutrition, which the doctor explained to me, saying that she was undernourished.

'She'll be better off and get proper food there,' said the landlady by way of comforting me.

She helped to gather up Mother's clothes and to dress her. Mother obeyed like a child; she was so weak, her will seemed to have deserted her. As we left the house, the neighbours and children were gathered at the front gate, looking on with awe.

The infirmary was about a mile away. As we ambled along Mother staggered like a drunken woman from weakness, veering from side to side as I supported her. The stark, afternoon sun seemed to ruthlessly expose our misery. People who passed us must have thought Mother was drunk, but to me they were like phantoms in a dream. She never spoke, but seemed to know where we were going and to be anxious to get there. On the way I tried to reassure her, and she smiled, too weak to talk.

When at last we arrived at the infirmary a young doctor took her in charge. After reading the note, he said kindly: 'All right, Mrs Chaplin, come this way.'

She submitted obediently. But as the nurses started to lead her away she turned suddenly with a painful realisation that she was leaving me behind.

'See you tomorrow,' I said, feigning cheerfulness.

They led her away looking anxiously back at me. When she had gone, the doctor turned. 'And what will become of you, young man?'

Having had enough of workhouse schools, I replied politely: 'Oh, I'll be living with my aunt.'

As I walked from the hospital towards home, I could feel only a numbing sadness. Yet I was relieved, for I knew that Mother would be better off in the hospital than sitting alone in that dark room with nothing to eat. But that heart-breaking look as they led her away I shall never forget. I thought of all her endearing ways, her gaiety, her sweetness and affection; of that weary little figure that used to come down the streets looking tired and preoccupied until she saw me charging towards her; how she would change immediately and become all smiling as I looked eagerly inside the paper bag she carried for those little niceties that she always brought home for Sydney and me. Even that morning she had saved some candy—had offered it to me while I wept in her lap.

I did not go straight home, I could not. I turned in the direction of the Newington Butts market and looked in shop windows until late afternoon. When I returned to the garret it looked reproachfully empty. On a chair was a wash-tub, half-filled with water. Two of my shirts and a chemise were soaking in it. I began to investigate; there was no food in the cupboard except a small half-filled package of tea. On the mantelpiece was her purse, in which I found three halfpence, some keys and several pawn tickets. On the corner of the table was the candy she had offered me. Then I broke down and wept again.

Emotionally exhausted, I slept soundly that night. In the morning I awoke to a haunting emptiness in the room; the sun streaming in on the floor seemed to heighten Mother's absence. Later the landlady came up and said that I could stay on there until she let the room and that if I needed food I had only to ask for it. I thanked her and told her that Sydney would pay all our debts when he returned. But I was too shy to ask for food.

I did not go to see Mother the next day as promised. I could not; it would have been too upsetting. But the landlady saw the doctor, who said that she had already been transferred to Cane Hill asylum. This melancholy news relieved my conscience, for Cane Hill was twenty miles away and I had no means of getting there. Sydney would soon return and then we could see her together. For the first few days I neither saw nor spoke to anyone I knew.

I would steal out in the early morning and stay out all day; I always managed to get food somewhere—besides, missing a meal was no hardship. One morning the landlady caught me creeping downstairs and asked if I had had my breakfast. I shook my head. 'Then come on,' she said in her gruff way.

I kept away from the McCarthys because I did not want them to know about Mother. Like a fugitive, I kept out of everyone's way.

*   *   *

It was one week since Mother had gone away, and I had settled into a precarious habit of living which I neither lamented nor enjoyed. My major concern was the landlady, for if Sydney did not return, sooner or later she would have to report me to the parish authorities and I would be sent again to Hanwell Schools. Thus I avoided her presence, even sleeping out occasionally.

I fell in with some wood-choppers who worked in a mews at the back of Kennington Road, derelict-looking men who worked hard in a darkened shed and spoke softly in undertones, sawing and chopping wood all day, making it into halfpenny bundles. I would hang about the open door and watch them. They would take a block of wood a foot square and chop it into inch slices and put these slices together and chop them into sticks. They chopped wood so rapidly that it fascinated me and made the job seem attractive. Very soon I was helping them. They bought their lumber from demolition contractors, and would cart it to their shed, stack it up, which took at least a day, then saw the wood one day and chop the next. On Friday and Saturday they would sell the firewood. But the selling of it did not interest me; it was more clubby working together in the shed.

They were affable, quiet men in their late thirties, but looked and acted much older. The boss (as we called him) had a diabetic red nose and no upper teeth except one fang. Yet there was a gentle sweetness about his face. He had a ridiculous grin that exposed prodigiously his one tooth. When short of an

70

extra tea-cup he would pick up an empty milk-tin, rinse it and, grinning, say: 'How's this for one?' The other man, though agreeable, was quiet, sallow-faced, thick-lipped and talked slowly. Around one o'clock the boss would look up at me: 'Have yer ever tasted Welsh rarebit made of cheese rinds?'

'We've had it many times,' I replied.

Then with a chortle and a grin he would give me twopence, and I would go to Ashe's, the tea grocers on the corner, who liked me and always gave me a lot for my money, and buy a pennyworth of cheese rinds and a pennyworth of bread. After washing and scraping the cheese we would add water and a little salt and pepper. Sometimes the boss would throw in a piece of bacon fat and a sliced onion, which together with a can of hot tea made a very appetising meal.

Although I never asked for money, at the end of the week the boss gave me sixpence, which was a pleasant surprise.

Joe, the sallow-faced one, suffered from fits and the boss would burn brown paper under his nose to bring him to. Sometimes he would foam at the mouth and bite his tongue, and when he recovered would look pathetic and ashamed.

The wood-choppers worked from seven in the morning until seven at night, sometimes later, and I always felt sad when they locked up the shed and went home. One night the boss decided to treat us to a twopenny gallery seat at the South London Music Hall. Joe and I were already washed and cleaned up, waiting for the boss. I was thrilled because Fred Karno's comedy *Early Birds* (the company I joined years later) was playing there that week. Joe was leaning against the wall of the mews and I was standing opposite him, enthusiastic and excited, when suddenly he let out a roar and slid down sideways against the wall in one of his fits. The anticipation had been too much. The boss wanted to stay and look after him, but Joe insisted that the two of us go without him and that he would be all right in the morning.

The threat of school was an ogre that never left me. Once in a while the wood-choppers would question me about it. They became a little uneasy when the holidays were over, so I would stay away from them until four-thirty, when school was let out. But it was a long, lonely day in the glare of incriminating streets, waiting until four-thirty to get back to my shadow retreat and the wood-choppers.

While I was creeping up to bed one night the landlady called me. She had been sitting up waiting. She was all excited and handed me a telegram. It read: 'Will arrive ten o'clock tomorrow morning at Waterloo Station. Love, Sydney.'

I was not an imposing sight to greet him at the station. My clothes were dirty and torn, my shoes yawned and the lining of my cap showed like a woman's dropping underskirt; and what face-washing I did was at the wood-choppers' tap, because it saved me having to carry a pail of water up three flights of stairs and pass the landlady's kitchen. When I met Sydney the shades of night were in my ears and around my neck.

Looking me over, he said: 'What's happened?'

I did not break the news too gently. 'Mother went insane and we had to send her to the infirmary.'

His face clouded, but he checked himself. 'Where are you living?'

'The same place, Pownall Terrace.'

He turned away to look after his baggage. I noticed he looked pale and gaunt. He ordered a brougham and the porters piled his luggage on top of it—amongst other things a crate of bananas!

'Is that ours?' I asked eagerly.

He nodded. 'They're too green; we'll have to wait a day or so before we can eat them.'

On the way home he began asking questions about Mother. I was too excited to give him a coherent account, but he got snatches. Then he told me he had been left behind in a hospital in Cape Town for medical treatment and that on the return trip he had made twenty pounds, money he looked forward to giving Mother. He had made it from the soldiers, organising sweepstakes and lotteries.

He told me of his plans. He intended giving up the sea and becoming an actor. He figured that the money would keep us for twenty weeks, in which time he would seek work in the theatre.

Our arrival in a cab with a crate of bananas impressed both the neighbours and the landlady. She told Sydney about Mother, but did not go into harrowing details.

The same day Sydney went shopping and outfitted me with new clothes, and that night, all dressed up, we sat in the stalls of the South London Music Hall. During the performance Sydney kept repeating: 'Just think what tonight would have meant to Mother.'

That week we went to Cane Hill to see her. As we sat in the visiting room, the ordeal of waiting became almost unbearable. I remember the keys turning and Mother walking in. She looked pale and her lips were blue, and, although she recognised us, it was without enthusiasm; her old ebullience had gone. She was accompanied by a nurse, an innocuous, glib woman, who stood and wanted to talk. 'It's a pity you came at such a time,' she said, 'for we're not quite ourselves today, are we, dear?'

Mother politely glanced at her and half smiled as though waiting for her to leave.

'You must come again when we're a little more up to the mark,' added the nurse.

Eventually she went, and we were left alone. Although Sydney tried to cheer Mother up, telling her of his good fortune and the money he had made and his reason for having been away so long, she just sat listening and nodding, looking vague and preoccupied. I told her that she would soon get well. 'Of course,' she said dolefully, 'if only you had given me a cup of tea that afternoon, I would have been all right.'

The doctor told Sydney afterwards that her mind was undoubtedly impaired by malnutrition, and that she required proper medical treatment, and that although she had lucid moments, it would be months before she completely recovered. But for days I was haunted by her remark: 'If only you had given me a cup of tea I would have been all right.'

V

JOSEPH CONRAD wrote to a friend to this effect: that life made him feel like a cornered blind rat waiting to be clubbed. This simile could well describe the appalling circumstances of us all; nevertheless, some of us are struck with good luck, and that is what happened to me.

I had been newsvendor, printer, toy-maker, glass-blower, doctor's boy etc., but during these occupational digressions, like Sydney, I never lost sight of my ultimate aim to become an actor. So between jobs I would polish my shoes, brush my clothes, put on a clean collar and make periodical calls at Blackmore's theatrical agency in Bedford Street off the Strand. I did this until the state of my clothes forbade any further visits.

The first time I went there, the office was adorned with immaculately dressed Thespians of both sexes, standing about talking grandiloquently to each other. With trepidation I stood in a far corner near the door, painfully shy, trying to conceal my weather-worn suit and shoes slightly budding at the toes. From the inner office a young clerk sporadically appeared and like a reaper would cut through the Thespian hauteur with the laconic remark: 'Nothing for you—or you—or you'—and the office would clear like the emptying of a church. On one occasion I was left standing alone! When the clerk saw me he stopped abruptly. 'What do you want?'

I felt like Oliver Twist asking for more. 'Have you any boys' parts?' I gulped.

'Have you registered?'

I shook my head.

To my surprise he ushered me into the adjoining office and took my name and address and all particulars, saying that if anything came up he would let me know. I left with a pleasant sense of having performed a duty, but also rather thankful that nothing had come of it.

And now one month after Sydney's return I received a post-card. It read: 'Would you call at Blackmore's agency, Bedford Street, Strand?'

In my new suit I was ushered into the very presence of Mr Blackmore himself, who was all smiles and amiability. Mr Blackmore, whom I had imagined to be all-mighty and scrutinising, was most kindly and gave me a note to deliver to Mr C. E. Hamilton at the offices of Charles Frohman.

Mr Hamilton read it and was amused and surprised to see how small I was. Of course I lied about my age, telling him I was fourteen—I was twelve and a half. He explained that I was to play Billie, the page-boy in *Sherlock Holmes*, for a tour of forty weeks which was to start in the autumn.

'In the meantime,' said Mr Hamilton, 'there is an exceptionally good boy's part in a new play *Jim, the Romance of a Cockney*, written by Mr H. A. Saintsbury, the gentleman who is to play the title role in *Sherlock Holmes* on the forthcoming tour.' *Jim* would be produced in Kingston for a trial engagement, prior to the tour of *Holmes*. The salary was two pounds ten shillings a week, the same as I would get for *Sherlock Holmes*.

Although the sum was a windfall I never batted an eye. 'I must consult my brother about the terms,' I said solemnly.

Mr Hamilton laughed and seemed highly amused, then brought out the whole office staff to have a look at me. 'This is our Billie! What do you think of him?'

Everyone was delighted and smiled beamingly at me. What had happened? It seemed the world had suddenly changed, had taken me into its fond embrace and adopted me. Then Mr Hamilton gave me a note to Mr Saintsbury, whom he said I would find at the Green Room Club in Leicester Square, and I left, walking on clouds.

The same thing happened at the Green Room Club, Mr Saintsbury calling out other members to have a look at me. Then and there he handed me the part of Sammy, saying that it was one of the important characters in his play. I was a little nervous for fear he might ask me to read it on the spot, which would have been embarrassing as I was almost unable to read; fortunately he told me to take it home and read it at leisure, as they would not be starting rehearsals for another week.

I went home on the bus dazed with happiness and began to get the full realisation of what had happened to me. I had suddenly left behind a life of poverty and was entering a long-desired dream—a dream my mother had often spoken about, had revelled in. I was to become an actor! It had all come so suddenly, so unexpectedly. I kept thumbing the pages of my part—it had a new brown paper cover—the most important document I have ever held in my life. During the ride on the bus I realised I had crossed an important threshold. No longer was I a nondescript of the slums; now I was a personage of the theatre. I wanted to weep.

Sydney's eyes were filmy when I told him what had happened. He sat crouched on the bed, thoughtfully looking out of the window, shaking and nodding his head; then said gravely: 'This is the turning point of our lives. If only Mother was here to enjoy it with us.'

'Think of it,' I continued, enthusiastically. 'Forty weeks at two pounds ten. I told Mr Hamilton you attended to all business matters, so,' I added eagerly, 'we might even get more. Anyway, we can save sixty pounds this year!'

After our enthusiasm had simmered down we reasoned that two pounds ten was hardly enough for such a big part. Sydney went to see if he could raise the ante—'there's no harm in trying,' I said—but Mr Hamilton was adamant. 'Two pounds ten is the maximum,' he said—and we were happy to get it.

Sydney read the part to me and helped me to memorise the lines. It was a big part, about thirty-five sides, but I knew it all by heart in three days.

The rehearsals of *Jim* took place in the upstairs foyer of the Drury Lane Theatre. Sydney had so zealously coached me that I was almost word-perfect. Only one word bothered me. The

77

line was: 'Who do you think you are—Mr Pierpont Morgan?' and I would say: 'Putterpint Morgan'. Mr Saintsbury made me keep it in. Those first rehearsals were a revelation. They opened up a new world of technique. I had no idea that there was such a thing as stage-craft, timing, pausing, a cue to turn, to sit, but it came naturally to me. Only one fault Mr Saintsbury corrected: I moved my head and 'mugged' too much when I talked.

After rehearsing a few scenes he was astonished and wanted to know if I had acted before. What a glow of satisfaction, pleasing Mr Saintsbury and the rest of the cast! However, I accepted their enthusiasm as though it were my natural birthright.

Jim was to be a try-out for one week at the Kingston Theatre and for another week at the Fulham. It was a melodrama patterned on Henry Arthur Jones's *Silver King*: the story of an aristocrat suffering from amnesia, who finds himself living in a garret with a young flower-girl and a newspaper boy, Sammy—my part. Morally, it was all on the up and up: the girl slept in the cupboard of the garret, while the Duke, as we called him, enjoyed the couch, and I slept on the floor.

The first act was at No 7A Devereux Court, the Temple, the chambers of James Seaton Gatlock, a wealthy lawyer. The tattered Duke, having called on his rival of a past love affair, begs for alms to help his sick benefactor, the flower-girl who had supported him during his amnesia.

In an altercation, the villain says to the Duke: 'Get out! Go and starve, you and your coster mistress!'

The Duke, though frail and weak, picks up a paper-knife from the desk as if to strike the villain, but it drops from his hands on to the desk as he is stricken with epilepsy, falling unconscious at the villain's feet. At this juncture, the villain's ex-wife, with whom the tattered Duke was once in love, enters the room. She also pleads for the tattered Duke, saying: 'He failed with me; he failed at the Bar! At least you can help him!'

But the villain refuses. The scene rises to a climax, in which he accuses his ex-wife of infidelity with the derelict and denounces her also. In a frenzy she picks up the paper-knife that fell from the derelict's hand and stabs the villain, who falls dead in his armchair, while the derelict still lies unconscious at his feet. The woman disappears from the scene, and the Duke, regaining consciousness, discovers his rival dead. 'God, what have I done?' says he.

Then business follows. He searches the dead man's pockets, finds a wallet in which he fingers several pounds, a diamond ring and jewellery, all of which he takes, and as he leaves by the window he turns, saying: 'Goodbye, Gatlock; you did help me, after all.' Curtain.

The next act was the garret in which the Duke lived. The scene opened with a lone detective looking into a cupboard. I enter whistling, then stop, seeing the detective.

NEWSBOY: Oi, you! Do you know that's a lady's bedroom?

DETECTIVE: What! That cupboard? Come here!

BOY: The cool cheek of him!

DETECTIVE: You stow that. Come in and shut the door.

BOY (*walking towards him*): Polite, ain't you, inviting blokes into their own drawing-room?

DETECTIVE: I'm a detective.

BOY: What, a cop? I'm off!

DETECTIVE: I'm not going to hurt you. All I want is a little information that will help to do someone a good turn.

BOY: A good turn indeed! If a bit of luck comes to anyone here, it won't be through the cops!

DETECTIVE: Don't be a fool. Would I have started by telling you I was in the Force?

BOY: Thanks for nothing. I can see your boots.

DETECTIVE: Who lives here?

BOY: The Duke.

DETECTIVE: Yes, but what's his real name?

BOY: I don't know. The Duke is a 'nom de guerre' as he calls it, though blow me if I know what it means.

DETECTIVE: And what does he look like?

BOY: As thin as a lath. Grey hair, clean shaven, wears a top hat and an eye-glass. And blimey, the way he looks at you through it!

DETECTIVE: And Jim—who's he?

BOY: He? You mean she!

DETECTIVE: Ah, then she's the lady who—

BOY (*interrupting*): Who sleeps in the cupboard—this here room's ours, mine and the Duke's, etc. etc.

There was much more to the part, and, believe it or not, it was highly amusing to the audience, due, I think, to my looking much younger than I was. Every line I spoke got a laugh. Only mechanics bothered me: the business of making real tea on the stage. I would 'get confused about whether to put the tea in the pot first or the hot water. Paradoxically enough, it was easier for me to talk lines than to carry out stage business.

Jim was not a success. The reviewers panned the play unmercifully. Nevertheless, I received favourable notices. One, which Mr Charles Rock, a member of our company, showed me, was exceptionally good. He was an old Adelphi actor of considerable reputation, and I played most of my scenes with him. 'Young man,' said he solemnly, 'don't get a swollen head when you read this.' And after lecturing me about modesty and graciousness he read the review of the *London Topical Times*, which I remember word for word. After writing disparagingly of the play it continued: 'But there is one redeeming feature, the part of Sammy, a newspaper boy, a smart London street Arab, much responsible for the comic part. Although hackneyed and old-fashioned, Sammy was made vastly amusing by Master Charles Chaplin, a bright and vigorous child actor. I have never heard of the boy before, but I hope to hear great things of him in the near future.' Sydney bought a dozen copies.

After completing the two weeks' run of *Jim*, we started rehearsals for *Sherlock Holmes*. During this time Sydney and I

When Little Charlie Chaplin Played in a Traveling English Road-Show

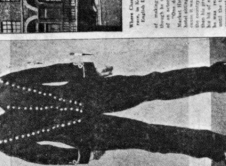

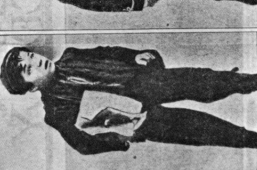

Charlie Chaplin at the Age of 15. Even Today This Picture Has Features That Have Become Familiar to Millions of Movie Patrons.

Charlie Chaplin as "Billy," the Newspaper-Boy Detective in "Sherlock Holmes," a Favorite English Stock Play When Chaplin Was a Lad of 14.

As a Page Boy in the Same Play. The Bellboy Suit Is One of "Billy's" Disguises in the Action of This Thriller.

Where Charlie Chaplin Was Born—No. 3 Parnell Terrace, in Kennington Road, One of a Row of Simple English Dwellings Built in the Nineteenth Century.

CHARLIE Chaplin, probably the most famous and one of the wealthiest of movie stars, has recently been revealed by a boyhood guardian as a person who always has taken his art with intense seriousness and who was bound to succeed because of his knack of making money and saving it.

This guardian, a former road-show actress, whose name is Miss Edith Scales and who now lives quietly in Scarborough, England, was moved by Chaplin's recent triumphal visit to England with his latest picture, to reminisce about the famous comedian's theatrical beginnings and some of the amusing things he did away back in 1904, when he was an ambitious young actor of fifteen.

"I first met Charlie," Miss Scales relates, "when he joined the road company which was touring England with Charles Frohman's Sherlock Holmes. There was no one to look after the boy so I took him under my wing.

"I remember one Saturday that Charlie was late for a matinee performance in which he was playing two parts, that of Billy, a newsboy detective, and of a page boy. When he finally arrived at the theatre and found that another boy was dressed in his clothes and on the stage, he broke out in tears and could not be comforted until the beginning of the second act, when he was allowed to resume his two roles.

"Even at the age of 15 Charlie was a hard-headed business man," said his onetime guardian. "To make extra money on the road he bought a five-shilling camera and, during his free time, used to go about, usually among groups of working people, snapping their pictures. He printed the photographs himself and sold them to his customers for threepence and sixpence each. He was n[illegible] afraid to work hard, and he looked upon no hones[illegible] of making money as beneath his dignity, even though he enjoyed the status and had the temperment of an actor.

"One day, when the company was staying at the Market Hotel, in Blackburn, Charlie noticed that the hotel sitting room was filled with farmers, in town because it was market day. He walked into the midst of the country folks and began singing songs in what was then his pronounced Cockney accent. And he finished his bit of entertainment by going into a clog dance—he was real clog dancer, too. His audience laughed until the tears streamed down their faces, but their amusement was somewhat lessened when Charlie circulated among them with his hat in his hand. He intended that his audience should pay for the impromptu show—and they did.

"Charlie wasn't mean, but he never threw away money unnecessarily. I recall how he used to check every item on the bills rendered him by landladies when we were on the road, and how he used to knock off items for service he hadn't been give[illegible] he had been out to tea one day during [illegible] he would deduct a proportiona[illegible] -bill.

"Everybody liked Charlie, though, [illegible] he was wonderfully clever. He de[illegible]

10. I played in *Sherlock Holmes* from 1901–5, in London and on tour. I remember I was very disappointed with these pictures of Billy when they were taken – I thought them extremely bad

11. Among the vaudeville turns I devised for myself at the age of sixteen was an impersonation of the well-known quack, 'Dr' Walford Brodie

12. I also liked to imitate the great Beerbohm Tree as Fagin in *Oliver Twist*

were still living at Pownall Terrace, because economically we were not too sure of our footing.

During rehearsals Sydney and I went to Cane Hill to see Mother. At first the nurses told us that she could not be seen as she was not well that day. They took Sydney aside out of my hearing, but I heard him say: 'No, I don't think he would.' Then turning to me sadly: 'You don't want to see Mother in a padded room?'

'No, no! I couldn't bear it!' I said, recoiling.

But Sydney saw her, and Mother recognised him and became rational. A few minutes later a nurse told me that Mother was well enough, if I wished to see her, and we sat together in her padded room. Before leaving she took me aside and whispered forlornly: 'Don't lose your way, because they might keep you here.' She remained eighteen months at Cane Hill before regaining her health. But Sydney saw her regularly while I was on tour.

*　　　*　　　*

Mr H. A. Saintsbury, who played Holmes on tour, was a living replica of the illustrations in the *Strand Magazine*. He had a long, sensitive face and an inspired forehead. Of all those who played Holmes he was considered the best, even better than William Gillette, the original Holmes and author of the play.

On my first tour, the management decided that I should live with Mr and Mrs Green, the carpenter of the company and his wife, the wardrobe lady. This was not very glamorous. Besides, Mr and Mrs Green drank occasionally. Moreover, I did not always want to eat when they did, or eat what they ate. I am sure my living with the Greens was more irksome to them than to me. So after three weeks we mutually agreed to part, and, being too young to live with other members of the cast, I lived alone. I was alone in strange towns, alone in back rooms, rarely meeting anyone until the evening performance, only hearing my own voice when I talked to myself. Occasionally, I would go to the saloons where members of the company gathered, and watch them play billiards; but I always felt that my presence cramped their conversation, and they were quite obvious in making me feel so. I could not smile at their levity without being frowned upon.

I began to grow melancholy. Arriving in northern towns on a Sunday night, hearing the doleful clanging of church bells as I walked the darkened main street, added little comfort to my loneliness. On week-days I would scan the local markets and do my shopping, buying groceries and meat for the landlady to cook. Sometimes I would get board and lodging, and eat in the kitchen with the family. I liked this, for north-country kitchens were clean and wholesome, with polished fire-grates and blue hearths. When the landlady baked bread, it was cheerful to come out of a cold dark day into the red glow of a Lancashire kitchen fire, and see tins of unbaked loaves around the hearth, and sit down to tea with the family—the taste of hot bread just out of the oven with fresh butter was relished with grave solemnity.

I had been in the provinces for six months. Meanwhile Sydney had had little success in getting a job in the theatre, so he was obliged to descend from his Thespian ambition and apply for a job as a bartender at the Coal Hole in the Strand. Out of one hundred and fifty applicants he got the job. But he had fallen ignominiously from his own graces, as it were.

He wrote to me regularly and kept me posted about Mother, but I seldom answered his letters; for one reason, I could not spell very well. One letter touched me deeply and drew me very close to him; he reproached me for not answering his letters and recalled the misery we had endured together which should unite us even closer. 'Since Mother's illness,' wrote Sydney, 'all we have in the world is each other. So you must write regularly and let me know that I have a brother.' His letter was so moving that I replied immediately. Now I saw

Sydney in another light. His letter cemented a brotherly love that has lasted throughout my life.

I got accustomed to living alone. But I got so much out of the habit of talking that when I suddenly met a member of the company I suffered intense embarrassment. I could not collect myself quickly enough to answer questions intelligently and they would leave me, I am sure, with alarm and concern for my reason. Miss Greta Hahn, for instance, our leading lady, was beautiful, charming and most kindly; yet when I saw her crossing the road towards me, I would quickly turn and look into a shop window or go down another street in order to avoid her.

I began to neglect myself and became desultory in my habits. When travelling with the company, I was always late at the railway station, arriving at the last moment, dishevelled and without a collar, and was continually reprimanded for it.

For company, I bought a rabbit and wherever I stayed I would smuggle it into my room unknown to the landlady. It was an endearing little thing, though not house-broken. Its fur looked so white and clean that it belied its pungent odour. I kept it in a wooden cage hidden under the bed. The landlady would cheerfully enter the room with my breakfast, until she contacted the odour, then she would leave, looking worried and confused. The moment she was gone I would release the rabbit and it would lope about the room.

Before long I had it trained to run to its box every time there was a knock at the door. If the landlady discovered my secret I would have the rabbit perform this trick, which usually won her heart, and she would put up with us for the week.

But in Tonypandy, Wales, after I showed my trick, the landlady smiled cryptically and made no comment; but when I returned from the theatre that night my pet had gone. When I enquired about it, the landlady merely shook her head. 'It must have run away or someone must have stolen it.' She had in her own way handled the problem efficaciously.

From Tonypandy we went to the mining town of Ebbw Vale, a three-night stand, and I was thankful it was not longer, for Ebbw Vale was a dank, ugly town in those days, with row upon row of hideous, uniform houses, each house consisting of four small rooms lit by oil-lamps. Most of the company put up at a small hotel. Fortunately I found a front room in a miner's house, and, though small, it was comfortable and clean. At night after the play my supper was left in front of the fire to keep warm.

The landlady, a tall, handsome, middle-aged woman, had an aura of tragedy about her. She came in in the morning with my breakfast and hardly spoke a word. I noticed that the kitchen door was always shut; whenever I wanted anything I had to knock, and the door opened only a few inches.

The second night, while I was having my supper, her husband came in, a man about the same age as his wife. He had been to the theatre that evening and had enjoyed the play. He stood a while conversing, holding a lighted candle, ready for bed. He came to a pause and seemed to think of what he wanted to say. 'Listen, I've got something that might fit your kind of business. Ever seen a human frog? Here, hold the candle and I'll take the lamp.'

He led the way into the kitchen and rested the lamp on the dresser, which had a curtain strung across the bottom of it in place of cupboard doors. 'Hey, Gilbert, come on out of there!' he said, parting the curtains.

A half a man with no legs, an oversized, blond, flat-shaped head, a sickening white face, a sunken nose, a large mouth and powerful muscular shoulders and arms, crawled from underneath the dresser. He wore flannel underwear with the legs of the garment cut off to the thighs, from which ten thick, stubby toes stuck out. The grisly creature could have been twenty or forty. He looked up and grinned, showing a set of yellow, widely spaced teeth.

'Hey, Gilbert, jump!' said the father and the wretched man

lowered himself slowly, then shot up by his arms almost to the height of my head.

'How do you think he'd fit in with a circus? The human frog!'

I was so horrified I could hardly answer. However, I suggested the names of several circuses that he might write to.

He insisted on the wretched creature going through further tricks, hopping, climbing and standing on his hands on the arms of a rocking chair. When at last he had finished I pretended to be most enthusiastic and complimented him on his tricks.

'Good-night, Gilbert,' I said before leaving, and in a hollow voice, and tongue-tied, the poor fellow answered: 'Good-night.'

Several times during the night I woke up and tried my locked door. The next morning the landlady seemed pleasant and communicative. 'I understand you saw Gilbert last night,' she said. 'Of course, he only sleeps under the dresser when we take in people from the theatre.'

Then the awful thought came to me that I had been sleeping in Gilbert's bed. 'Yes,' I answered, and talked with measured enthusiasm of the possibilities of his joining a circus.

She nodded. 'We have often thought of it.'

My enthusiasm—or whatever it was—seemed to please the landlady, and before leaving I went into the kitchen to say goodbye to Gilbert. With an effort to be casual I shook his large calloused hand, and he gently shook mine.

*   *   *

After forty weeks in the provinces, we returned to play eight weeks around the suburbs of London. *Sherlock Holmes*, being a phenomenal success, was to start a second tour, three weeks after the finish of the first one.

Now Sydney and I decided to give up our quarters in Pownall Terrace and take up more respectable ones in the

Kennington Road; like snakes we wanted to slough our skins, shedding every vestige of the past.

I spoke to the management about Sydney for a small part in the next tour of *Holmes*, and he got it—thirty-five shillings a week! Now we were on tour together.

Sydney wrote to Mother every week and towards the end of our second tour we received a letter from Cane Hill asylum stating that she had fully recovered her health. This was indeed good news. Quickly we made arrangements for her discharge, and made preparations for her to join us in Reading. To celebrate the occasion we took a special apartment de luxe, consisting of two bedrooms and a sitting-room with a piano, fixed up her bedroom with flowers, and arranged an elaborate dinner to boot.

Sydney and I waited for her at the railroad station, tense and happy, yet I could not help feeling anxious as to how she would fit into our lives again, knowing that the close ties of other days could never be recaptured.

At last the train arrived. With excitement and uncertainty we scanned the faces of the passengers as they left the carriages. Then at last there she was, smiling and walking sedately towards us. She displayed no great emotion as we went to meet her, but greeted us with affectionate decorum. She evidently was also undergoing an adjustment.

In that short ride in a cab to our rooms, we talked of a hundred different things, relevant and irrelevant.

After the first flush of enthusiasm of showing her the apartment and the flowers in the bedroom, we found ourselves in the sitting-room looking breathlessly at each other. It was a sunny day, and our apartment was on a quiet street, but now the silence of it was uncomfortable and in spite of my wanting to be happy I found myself fighting back a depression. Poor Mother, who wanted so little out of life to make her gay and cheerful, reminded me of my unhappy past—the last person in the world who should have affected me this way. But I did my best to hide the fact. She had aged a little and gained weight. I had always been proud of the way Mother looked and dressed and wanted to show her off to the company at her best, but now she appeared rather dowdy. She must have sensed my misgivings, for she turned enquiringly.

Coyly I adjusted a strand of her hair. 'Before you meet the company,' I smiled, 'I want you to be at your best.'

She looked at me, then took out her powder-puff and rubbed it over her face. 'I'm just happy to be alive,' she said cheerfully.

It was not long before we were fully adjusted to one another and my dejection passed. That we had outgrown the intimacy she had known when we were children, she understood better than we did, which made her all the more endearing to us. On tour she did the shopping and catering, bringing home fruits and delicacies and always a few flowers. For no matter how poor we had been in the past, when shopping on Saturday nights she had always been able to buy a pennyworth of wallflowers. Occasionally she was quiet and reserved, and her detachment saddened me. She acted more like a guest than our mother.

After a month she wanted to return to London, because she was anxious to get settled down so that she would have a home for us after our tour; besides, as she said, it would be less costly than travelling over the country and having to pay an extra fare.

She rented the flat over the barber's shop in Chester Street where we had once lived, and with ten pounds bought furniture on the instalment plan. The rooms had not the spaciousness of Versailles, or its elegance; but she did wonders in the bedrooms by covering orange-crates with cretonne to make them look like commodes. Between us Sydney and I were earning four pounds five shillings a week and sending one pound five shillings of it to Mother.

Sydney and I returned home after our second tour and spent a few weeks with her. Although we were happy to be with Mother, we were secretly glad to get away on tour again, for

Chester Street had not the requisite comforts that provincial apartments had—those little amenities to which Sydney and I were now accustomed. And Mother no doubt realised this. When she saw us off at the station she seemed cheerful enough, but we both thought she looked wistful as she stood on the platform smiling and waving her handkerchief as the train pulled away.

During our third tour Mother wrote to us that Louise, with whom Sydney and I had lived in the Kennington Road, had died, ironically enough, in the Lambeth workhouse, the same place, in which we had been confined. She survived Father only by four years, leaving her little son an orphan, and he also had been sent to the same Hanwell Schools that Sydney and I had been sent to.

Mother wrote that she had visited the boy, explaining who she was, and that Sydney and I had lived with him and his father and mother in the Kennington Road. But he hardly remembered, as he had been only four years old at the time. He also had no recollection of his father. And now he was ten. He was registered under Louise's maiden name, and as far as Mother could find out he had no relatives. She described him as being a handsome boy, very quiet, shy and preoccupied. She brought him a bag of sweets and some oranges and apples and promised to visit him regularly, which I believe she did, until she herself became ill again and was sent back to Cane Hill.

The news of Mother's relapse came like a stab in the heart. We never knew the details. We received only a curt official notice that she had been found wandering and incoherent in the streets. There was nothing we could do but accept poor Mother's fate. She never again recovered her mind completely. For several years she languished in Cane Hill asylum until we could afford to put her into a private one.

Sometimes the gods of adversity tire of their sport and show mercy, as they did with Mother. For the last seven years of her life she was to live in comfort, surrounded by flowers and sunshine, to see her grown sons endowed with fame and fortune beyond anything she had ever imagined.

* * *

Because of our tour with *Sherlock Holmes* it was many weeks before Sydney and I could again see Mother. The tour with the Frohman company ended permanently. Then Mr Harry York, proprietor of the Theatre Royal, Blackburn, bought the rights of *Holmes* from Frohman to play the smaller towns. Sydney and I were engaged by the new company, but at reduced salaries of thirty-five shillings each.

It was a depressing come-down, playing the small towns of the North with an inferior company. Nevertheless, it enlivened my discrimination, comparing the company with the one we had just left. This comparison I tried to conceal, but at rehearsals in my zeal to help the new director, who would ask me about stage directions, cues and business etc., I would eagerly tell him how it was done in the Frohman company. This, of course, did not make me particularly popular with the cast and I was looked upon as a precocious brat. Later, a new stage manager had it in for me and fined me ten shillings for having a button missing from my uniform, about which he had warned me several times.

William Gillette, author of *Sherlock Holmes*, came to London with Marie Doro in a play called *Clarissa* which he had written. The critics were unkind to the play and to the manner of Gillette's speech, which led him to write a curtain-raiser, *The Painful Predicament of Sherlock Holmes*, in which he himself never spoke a word. There were only three in the cast, a mad-woman, Holmes and his page-boy. It was like tidings from heaven to receive a telegram from Mr Postant, Gillette's manager, asking if I were available to come to London to play the part of Billie with William Gillette in the curtain-raiser.

I trembled with anxiety, for it was doubtful if our company could replace Billie in the provinces on such short notice, and for several days I was left in agonising suspense. However, they did find another Billie.

Returning to London to play in a West End theatre I can only describe as my renaissance. My brain was spinning with the thrill of every incident—arriving in the evening at the Duke of York's Theatre and meeting Mr Postant, the stage manager, who brought me to Mr Gillette's dressing-room, and his words after I was introduced to him: 'Would you like to play in *Sherlock Holmes* with me?' And my burst of nervous enthusiasm: 'Oh very much, Mr Gillette!' And the next morning, waiting on the stage for rehearsals, and seeing Marie Doro for the first time, dressed in the loveliest white summer dress. The sudden shock of seeing someone so beautiful at that hour! She had been riding in a hansom cab and had discovered an ink spot on her dress, and wanted to know if the property man had anything that would take it out, and to his answer of doubt she made the prettiest expression of irritation: 'Oh, isn't that too beastly!'

She was so devastatingly beautiful that I resented her. I resented her delicate, pouting lips, her regular white teeth, her adorable chin, her raven hair and dark brown eyes. I resented her pretence of irritation and the charm she exuded through it. Through all this querying between herself and the property man she was ignorant of my presence, although I stood quite near, staring, transfixed by her beauty. I had just turned sixteen, and the propinquity of this sudden radiance evoked my determination not to be obsessed by it. But, oh God, she was beautiful! It was love at first sight.

In *The Painful Predicament of Sherlock Holmes* Miss Irene Vanbrugh, a remarkably gifted actress, played the madwoman and did all the talking, while Holmes just sat and listened. This was his joke on the critics. I had the opening lines, bursting into Holmes's apartment and holding on to the doors while the madwoman beats against them outside, and then, while I excitedly try to explain to Holmes the situation, the madwoman bursts in! For twenty minutes she never stops raving incoherently about some case that she wants him to solve. Surreptitiously Holmes writes a note, rings a bell and slips it to me. Later two stalwart men lead the lady off, leaving Holmes and me alone, with me saying: 'You were right, sir; it was the right asylum.'

The critics enjoyed the joke, but the play *Clarissa*, which Gillette wrote for Marie Doro, was a failure. Although they raved about Marie's beauty, they said it was not enough to hold a maudlin play together, so he completed the rest of his season with the revival of *Sherlock Holmes*, in which I was retained for the part of Billie.

In my excitement to play with the famous William Gillette, I had forgotten to ask about terms. At the end of the week Mr Postant came apologetically with my pay envelope. 'I'm really ashamed to give you this,' he said, 'but at the Frohman office they said I was to pay you the same as you were getting with us before: two pounds ten.' I was agreeably surprised.

At rehearsals of *Holmes*, I met Marie Doro again—more beautiful than ever!—and in spite of my resolutions not to be overwhelmed by her, I began to sink further into the hopeless mire of silent love. I hated this weakness and was furious with myself for lack of character. It was an ambivalent affair. I both hated and loved her. What's more, she was charming and gracious to boot.

In *Holmes* she played Alice Faulkner, but in the play we never met. I would wait, however, timing the moment when I could pass her on the stairs and gulp 'Good-evening', and she would answer cheerfully 'Good-evening'. And that was all that ever passed between us.

Holmes was an immediate success. During the engagement Queen Alexandra saw the play; sitting with her in the Royal Box were the King of Greece and Prince Christian. The Prince was evidently explaining the play to the King and during the most tense and silent moment, when Holmes and

I were alone on the stage, a booming voice with an accent resounded throughout the theatre: 'Don't tell me! Don't tell me!'

Dion Boucicault had his offices in the Duke of York's Theatre, and in passing he would give me an approving little tap on the head; as did Hall Caine, who frequently came back stage to see Gillette. On one occasion, I also received a smile from Lord Kitchener.

During the run of *Sherlock Holmes*, Sir Henry Irving died and I attended the funeral at Westminster Abbey. Being a West End actor, I was given a special pass and I felt very proud of the fact. At the funeral, I sat between the solemn Lewis Waller, then the romantic matinée idol of London, and 'Dr' Walford Bodie of bloodless surgery fame, whom I later burlesqued in a vaudeville skit. Waller looked handsomely profiled for the occasion, sitting stiffly, looking neither right nor left. But 'Dr' Bodie, in order to get a better view as they lowered Sir Henry into the crypt, kept stepping on the chest of a supine duke, much to the indignation and contempt of Mr Waller. I gave up trying to see anything and sat down, resigned to viewing the backsides of those in front of me.

Two weeks before the ending of *Sherlock Holmes*, Mr Boucicault gave me a letter of introduction to the illustrious Mr and Mrs Kendal, with the prospects of getting a part in their new play. They were terminating a successful run at the St James's Theatre. The appointment was for ten a.m., to meet the lady in the foyer of the theatre. She was twenty minutes late. Eventually, a silhouette appeared off the street: it was Mrs Kendal, a stalwart, imperious lady, who greeted me with: 'Oh, so you're the boy! We are shortly to begin a tour of the provinces in a new play, and I'd like to hear you read for the part. But at the moment we are very busy. So will you be here tomorrow morning at the same time?'

'I'm sorry, madam,' I replied coldly, 'but I cannot accept anything out of town.' And with that I raised my hat, walked out of the foyer, hailed a passing cab—and was out of work for ten months.

The night *Sherlock Holmes* ended its run at the Duke of York's Theatre and Marie Doro was to return to America, I went off alone and got desperately drunk. Two or three years later in Philadelphia, I saw her again. She dedicated the opening of a new theatre in which I was playing in Karno's comedy company. She was still as beautiful as ever. I stood in the wings watching her in my comedy make-up while she made a speech, but I was too shy to make myself known to her.

At the closing of *Holmes* in London the company in the provinces also ended, so both Sydney and I were out of work. But Sydney lost no time in getting another job. As a result of seeing an advertisement in the *Era*, a theatrical paper, he joined Charlie Manon's troupe of knockabout comedians. In those days there were several of these troupes touring the halls: Charlie Baldwin's Bank Clerks, Joe Boganny's Lunatic Bakers, and the Boicette troupe, all of them pantomimists. And although they played slapstick comedy, it was performed to beautiful music *à la ballet* and was most popular. The outstanding company was Fred Karno's, who had a large repertoire of comedies. Each one was called 'Birds'. There were *Jail Birds*, *Early Birds*, *Mumming Birds*, etc. From these three sketches Karno built a theatrical enterprise of more than thirty companies, whose repertoire included Christmas pantomimes and elaborate musical comedies, from which he developed such fine artists and comedians as Fred Kitchen, George Graves, Harry Weldon, Billie Reeves, Charlie Bell and many others.

It was while Sydney was working with the Manon troupe that Fred Karno saw him and signed him up at a salary of four pounds a week. Being four years younger than Sydney, I was neither fish nor fowl for any form of theatrical work, but I had saved a little money from the London engagement and while Sydney was working in the provinces I stayed in London and played around pool-rooms.

VI

I HAD arrived at that difficult and unattractive age of adolescence, conforming to the teenage emotional pattern. I was a worshipper of the foolhardy and the melodramatic, a dreamer and a moper, raging at life and loving it, a mind in a chrysalis yet erupting with sudden bursts of maturity. In this labyrinth of distorting mirrors I dallied, my ambition going in spurts. The word 'art' never entered my head or my vocabulary. The theatre meant a livelihood and nothing more.

Through this haze and confusion I lived alone. Whores, sluts and an occasional drinking bout weaved in and out of this period, but neither wine, women nor song held my interest for long. I really wanted romance and adventure.

I can well understand the psychological attitude of the teddy boy with his Edwardian dress; like all of us he wants attention, romance and drama in his life. Why should he not indulge in moments of exhibitionism and horseplay, as does the public-school boy with his gadding and ragging? Is it not natural that when he sees the so-called better classes asserting their foppery he wants to assert his own?

He knows that the machine obeys his will as it does the will of any class; that it requires no special mentality to shift a gear or press a button. In this insensate age is he not as formidable as any Lancelot, aristocrat or scholar, his finger as powerful in destroying a city as any Napoleonic army? Is not the teddy boy a phoenix rising from the ashes of a delinquent ruling class, his attitude perhaps motivated by a subconscious feeling: that man is only a half-tame animal who has for generations governed others by deceit, cruelty and violence? But, as Bernard Shaw said: 'I am digressing as a man with a grievance always does'.

I eventually obtained work with a vaudeville sketch, Casey's Circus, doing a burlesque on Dick Turpin, the highwayman, and 'Dr' Walford Bodie. With 'Dr' Bodie I had a modicum of success, for it was more than just low comedy; it was a characterisation of a professorial, scholarly man, and I conceived the happy idea of making up to look exactly like him. I was the star of the company, and earned three pounds a week. It included a troupe of kids playing at grown-ups in an alley scene; it was an awful show, I thought, but it gave me a chance to develop as a comedian.

When Casey's Circus played in London, six of us boarded in the Kennington Road with Mrs Fields, an old widowed lady of sixty-five, who had three daughters: Frederica, Thelma and Phoebe. Frederica was married to a Russian cabinet-maker, a gentle but an extremely ugly man, with a broad Tartar face, blond hair, blond moustache and a cast in his eye. The six of us ate in the kitchen, and we got to know the family very well. Sydney when working in London also lived there.

When eventually I left Casey's Circus, I returned to Kennington Road and continued to board with the Fields. The old lady was kindly, patient and hard-working and her sole income came from renting rooms. Frederica, the married daughter, was supported by her husband. Thelma and Phoebe helped with the housework. Phoebe was fifteen and beautiful. Her features were long and aquiline, and she had a strong appeal for me both physically and sentimentally; the latter I resisted because I was not quite seventeen and had only the worst of intentions about girls. But she was saintly and nothing ever came of it. She grew fond of me, however, and we became very good friends.

The Fields were an intensely emotional family and would occasionally break out into passionate quarrelling with each other. The basis of contention was usually whose turn it was to do the housework. Thelma, who was about twenty, was the lady of the family and the lazy one, and always claimed that it was Frederica's or Phoebe's turn. This would develop from an argument into a brawl, in which buried grievances and family

95

skeletons were hewed up and cast about for all to view. Mrs Fields revealing the fact that since Thelma had run off and lived with a young Liverpool lawyer she thought she was a lady and that she was too good to do housework, climaxing her tirade by saying: 'Well, if you're such a lady, clear out and go back and live with your Liverpool lawyer—only he won't have you.' And for final emphasis Mrs Fields would pick up a teacup and smash it on the floor. During this Thelma would sit at the table, ladylike and unperturbed. Then calmly she would take a cup and do likewise, lightly dropping it on the floor, saying: 'I too, can lose my temper,' dropping another cup, then another, then another and another until the floor was strewn with broken crockery. 'I, too, can make a scene.' And the poor mother and the sisters would look on helplessly. 'Look at her! Look what she's doing!' moaned the mother. 'Here! Here's something else you can smash,' handing Thelma the sugar-bowl, and Thelma would take it and calmly drop it.

On these occasions Phoebe was the arbitrator. She was fair and just and had the respect of the family, and she would usually end the argument by offering to do the work herself, which Thelma would not allow her to do.

I had been out of work for almost three months and Sydney had been supporting me, paying Mrs Fields fourteen shillings a week for my board and lodgings. He was now a leading comedian with Fred Karno, and had often spoken to Karno about his talented young brother, but Karno turned a deaf ear, because he thought I was too young.

At the time Jewish comedians were all the rage in London, so I thought I would hide my youth under whiskers. Sydney gave me two pounds, which I invested in musical arrangements for songs and funny dialogue taken from an American joke-book, *Madison's Budget*. For weeks I practised, performing in front of the Fields family. They were attentive and encouraging but nothing more.

I had obtained a trial week without pay at the Foresters'

13. Mr and Mrs Fred Karno (left) on their houseboat at Tagg's Island

14. My brother Sydney

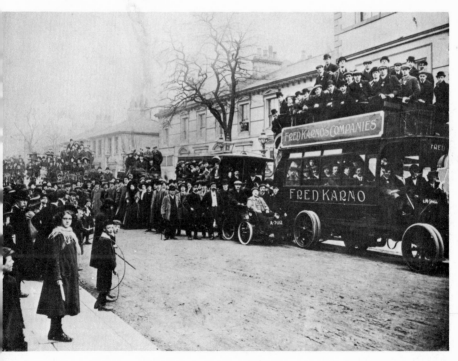

15. Five companies outside Karno's office in Camberwell leaving for the music halls in and around London

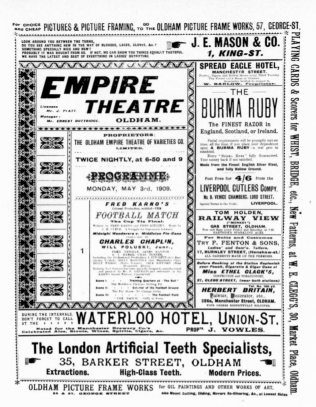

16. A poster advertising Fred Karno's
'Colossal Production' of *The Football Match*

17. Marie Doro in *Sherlock Holmes*

18. When I was nineteen I fell in love
for the first time. Hetty Kelly was
fifteen. I met her at the Streatham
Empire where I was playing the drunk
in *Mumming Birds* and she was with a
song-and-dance troupe

Music Hall, which was a small theatre situated off the Mile End Road in the centre of the Jewish quarter. I had played there previously with Casey's Circus and the management thought I was good enough to be given a chance. My future hopes and dreams depended on that trial week. After the Foresters' I would play all the important circuits in England. Who knows ? Within a year I might rise to be one of vaudeville's biggest headliners. I had promised the whole Fields family that I would get them tickets towards the end of the week, when I was thoroughly at home with my act.

'I suppose you won't want to live with us after your success,' said Phoebe.

'Of course I will,' I said graciously.

Twelve o'clock Monday morning was band rehearsal for songs and cues etc., which I carried out professionally. But I had not given sufficient thought to my make-up. I was undecided how I should look. For hours before the night show I was in the dressing-room experimenting, but no matter how much crêpe hair I used I could not hide my youth. Although I was innocent of it, my comedy was most anti-Semitic, and my jokes were not only old ones but very poor, like my Jewish accent. Moreover, I was not funny.

After the first couple of jokes the audience started throwing coins and orange-peel and stamping their feet and booing. At first I was not conscious of what was going on. Then the horror of it filtered into my mind. I began to hurry and talk faster as the jeers, the raspberries, and the throwing of coins and orange-peel increased. When I came off the stage, I did not wait to hear the verdict from the management; I went straight to the dressing-room, took off my make-up, left the theatre and never returned, not even to collect my music books.

It was late when I returned home to Kennington Road and the Fields family had all gone to bed, and I was thankful they had. In the morning at breakfast Mrs Fields was anxious to know how the show went. I bluffed indifference and said: 'All

97

right, but it needs a few alterations.' She said that Phoebe had gone to see me, but had told them nothing, as she was too tired and wanted to get to bed. When I saw Phoebe later she did not mention it, neither did I; nor did Mrs Fields or any of the family ever mention it again, or show any surprise at my not continuing the week.

Thank God Sydney was in the provinces, so I had not the painful ordeal of telling him what had happened—but he must have guessed, or the Fields might have told him, because he never did enquire about it. I did my best to erase that night's horror from my mind, but it left an indelible mark on my confidence. That ghastly experience taught me to see myself in a truer light; I realised I was not a vaudeville comedian, I had not that intimate, come-hither faculty with an audience; and I consoled myself with being a character comedian. However, I was to have one or two more disappointments before landing on my professional feet.

At seventeen I played a juvenile lead in a sketch called *The Merry Major*, a cheap, depressing affair lasting only a week. The leading lady, my wife, was a woman of fifty. Each night she reeled on to the stage smelling of gin, and I, the enthusiastic, loving husband, would have to take her in my arms and kiss her. That experience weaned me away from any ambition to be a leading man.

Then I tried authorship. I wrote a comedy sketch called *Twelve Just Men*, a slapstick affair about a jury arguing a case of breach of promise. One of the jury was a deaf-mute, another a drunk and another a quack doctor. I sold the idea to Charcoate, a vaudeville hypnotist who would hypnotise a stooge and make him drive through the town in a landau, blindfold, while he sat in the back throwing magnetic impulses at him. He gave me three pounds for my script, providing I directed it. We engaged a cast and rehearsed over the Horns public house clubrooms in the Kennington Road. One disgruntled old actor said that the sketch was not only illiterate but silly.

The third day, in the middle of rehearsals, I received a note from Charcoate to say he had decided not to produce it. Not being the valiant type, I put the note in my pocket and went on rehearsing. I had not the courage to tell the cast. Instead, at lunch-time, I took them home to our rooms and told them my brother wished to talk to them. I took Sydney into the bedroom and showed him the note. After reading it he said: 'Well, didn't you tell them?'

'No,' I whispered.

'Well, tell them.'

'I can't,' I said. 'I just can't, after their having rehearsed three days for nothing.'

'But that's not your fault,' said Sydney. 'Go and tell them,' he shouted.

I lost courage and began to weep. 'What can I say?'

'Don't be a fool!' He got up and went into the next room and showed them Charcoate's letter, explaining what had happened, then he took us all to the corner pub for a sandwich and a drink.

Actors are unpredictable. The old chap who had grumbled so much was the most philosophical, and laughed when Sydney told him of the awful state I was in. 'It's not your fault, sonny,' he said, patting me on the back. 'It's that bloody old scoundrel, Charcoate.'

*   *   *

After my failure at the Foresters', everything I attempted met with disaster. However, a most formidable element in optimism is youth, for it instinctively feels that adversity is *pro tem* and that a continual run of ill luck is just as implausible as the straight and narrow path of righteousness. Both eventually must deviate.

My luck changed. One day Sydney told me that Mr Karno wanted to see me. It appears he was dissatisfied with one of the comedians playing opposite Mr Harry Weldon in *The Football Match*, one of Karno's most successful sketches. Weldon was a very popular comedian who remained popular up to the time of his death in the 'thirties.

Mr Karno was a thick-set, bronzed little man, with keen sparkling eyes that were always appraising. He had started as an acrobat on the horizontal bars, then got together three knock-about comedians. This quartette was the nucleus of his comedy pantomime sketches. He himself was an excellent comedian and originated many comedy roles. He continued playing even when he had five other companies on the road.

One of the original members tells the story of his retirement. One night in Manchester, after a performance, the troupe complained that Karno's timing was off and that he had ruined the laughs. Karno, who had then accumulated £50,000 from his five shows, said: 'Well, boys, if that's the way you feel, I'll quit!' then, taking off his wig, he dropped it on the dressing-table and grinned. 'You can accept that as my resignation.'

Mr Karno's home was in Coldharbour Lane, Camberwell; annexed to it was a warehouse in which he stored the scenery for his twenty productions. He also maintained his offices there. When I arrived he received me kindly. 'Sydney's been telling me how good you are,' he said. 'Do you think you could play opposite Harry Weldon in *The Football Match*?'

Harry Weldon was specially engaged at a high salary, getting thirty-four pounds a week.

'All I need is the opportunity,' I said confidently.

He smiled. 'Seventeen's very young, and you look even younger.'

I shrugged off-handedly. 'That's a question of make-up.'

Karno laughed. That shrug, he told Sydney later, got me the job.

'Well, well, we'll see what you can do,' he said.

It was to be a trial engagement of two weeks at three pounds ten a week, and if I proved satisfactory I would get a year's contract.

*　　　　*　　　　*

I had a week to study the part before opening at the London Coliseum. Karno told me to go to Shepherd's Bush Empire, where *The Football Match* was playing, and to watch the man whose part I was to play. I must confess he was dull and self-conscious and, without false modesty, I knew that I had him beat. The part needed more burlesque. I made up my mind to play him just that way.

I was given only two rehearsals, as Mr Weldon was not available for more; in fact, he was rather annoyed at having to show up at all because it broke into his game of golf.

At rehearsals I was not impressive. Being a slow reader, I felt that Weldon had reservations about my competence. Sydney, having played the same part, might have helped me had he been in London, but he was playing in the provinces in another sketch.

Although *The Football Match* was a burlesque slapstick affair, there was not a laugh in it until Weldon appeared. Everything led up to his entrance, and of course Weldon, excellent comedian that he was, kept the audience in continuous laughter from the moment he came on.

On the opening night at the Coliseum my nerves were wound tight like a clock. That night meant re-establishing my confidence and wiping out the disgrace of that nightmare at the Foresters'. At the back of the enormous stage I walked up and down, with anxiety superimposed on fear, praying to myself.

There was the music! The curtain rose! On the stage was a chorus of men exercising. Eventually they exited, leaving the stage empty. That was my cue. In an emotional chaos I went on. One either rises to an occasion or succumbs to it. The moment I walked on to the stage I was relieved, everything was clear. I entered with my back to the audience—an idea of my own. From the back I looked immaculate, dressed in a frock-coat, top-hat, cane and spats—a typical Edwardian villain. Then I turned, showing my red nose. There was a laugh. That ingratiated me with the audience. I shrugged melo-dramatically, then snapped my fingers and veered across the stage, tripping over a dumb-bell. Then my cane became entangled with an upright punching bag, which rebounded and slapped me in the face. I swaggered and swung, hitting myself with my cane on the side of the head. The audience roared.

Now I was relaxed and full of invention. I could have held the stage for five minutes and kept them laughing without uttering a word. In the midst of my villainous strutting my trousers began to fall down. I had lost a button. I began looking for it. I picked up an imaginary something, then indignantly threw it aside: 'Those confounded rabbits!' Another laugh.

Harry Weldon's head came round the wings like a full moon. There had never been a laugh before he came on.

When he made his entrance I dramatically grabbed his wrist and whispered: 'Quick! I'm undone! A pin!' All this was *ad lib* and unrehearsed. I had conditioned the audience well for Harry, he was a tremendous success that evening and to-gether we added many extra laughs. When the curtain came down, I knew I had made good. Several members of the troupe shook hands and congratulated me. On the way to the dressing-room, Weldon looked over his shoulder and said dryly: 'That was all right—fine!'

That night I walked home to get unwound. I paused and leaned over Westminster Bridge and watched the dark, silky waters drifting under it. I wanted to weep for joy, but I couldn't. I kept straining and grimacing, but no tears would come, I was empty. From Westminster Bridge I walked to the Elephant and Castle and stopped at a coffee-stall for a cup of tea. I wanted to talk to someone, but Sydney was in the provinces. If only he were here so that I could tell him about tonight, how much it all meant to me, especially after the Foresters'.

I could not sleep. From the Elephant and Castle I went on to Kennington Gate and had another cup of tea. On the way I kept talking and laughing to myself. It was five in the morning before I got to bed, exhausted.

Mr Karno was not there the first night, but came the third, on which occasion I received applause when I made my entrance. He came round afterwards, all smiles, and told me to come to his office in the morning and sign the contract.

I had not written to Sydney about the first night, but sent him a succinct wire: 'Have signed contract for one year at four pounds per week. Love, Charlie.' *The Football Match* stayed in London fourteen weeks, then went on tour.

Weldon's comedy character was of the cretinous type, a slow-speaking Lancashire boob. That went very well in the North of England, but in the South he was not too well received. Bristol, Cardiff, Plymouth, Southampton, were slump towns for Weldon; during those weeks he was irritable and performed perfunctorily and took his spleen out on me. In the show he had to slap and knock me about quite a bit. This was called 'taking the nap', that is, he would pretend to hit me in the face, but someone would slap their hands in the wings to give it a realistic effect. Sometimes he really slapped me and unnecessarily hard, provoked, I think, by jealousy.

In Belfast the situation came to a head. The critics had given Weldon a dreadful panning, but had praised my performance. This was intolerable to Weldon, so that night on the stage he let me have a good one which took all the comedy out of me and made my nose bleed. Afterwards I told him that if he did it again I would brain him with one of the dumb-bells on the stage, and added that if he was jealous, not to take it out on me.

'Jealous of you,' said he contemptuously, on our way to the dressing-room. 'Why, I have more talent in my arse than you have in your whole body!'

'That's where your talent lies,' I retorted, and quickly closed the dressing-room door.

*   *   *

When Sydney came to town we decided to get a flat in the Brixton Road and to furnish it to the extent of forty pounds. We went to a second-hand furniture shop in Newington Butts and told the owner how much we could afford to spend, and that we had four rooms to furnish. The owner took a personal interest in our problem and spent many hours helping us pick out bargains. We carpeted the front room and linoleumed the others and bought an upholstered suite—a couch and two armchairs. In one corner of the sitting-room we put a fretwork Moorish screen, lighted from behind by a coloured yellow bulb, and in the opposite corner, on a gilt easel, a pastel in a gilded frame. The picture was of a nude model standing on a pedestal, looking sideways over her shoulder as a bearded artist is about to brush a fly off her bottom. This *objet d'art* and the screen, I thought, made the room. The final décor was a combination of a Moorish cigarette shop and a French whore-house. But we loved it. We even bought an upright piano, and although we spent fifteen pounds over our budget, we certainly had value for it. The flat at 15 Glenshaw Mansions, Brixton Road, was our cherished haven. How we looked forward to it after playing in the provinces! We were now prosperous enough to help Grandfather and give him ten shillings a week and we were able to engage a maid to come twice a week and clean up the flat, but it was hardly necessary, for we rarely disturbed a thing. We lived in it as though it were a holy temple. Sydney and I would sit in our bulky armchairs with smug satisfaction. We had bought a raised brass fender with red leather seating around it and I would go from the armchair to the fender, testing them for comfort.

*   *   *

At sixteen my idea of romance had been inspired by a theatrical poster showing a girl standing on a cliff with the wind blowing through her hair. I imagined myself playing golf with her—a game I loathe—walking over the dewy downs, indulging in throbbing sentiment, health and nature. That was romance. But young love is something else. It usually follows a uniform pattern. Because of a glance, a few words at the beginning (usually asinine words), in a matter of minutes the whole aspect of life is changed, all nature is in sympathy with us, and suddenly reveals its hidden joys. And that is what happened to me.

I was almost nineteen and already a successful comedian in the Karno Company, but something was lacking. Spring had come and gone and summer was upon me with an emptiness. My daily routine was stale, my environment dreary. I could see nothing in my future but a commonplaceness among dull, commonplace people. To be occupied with the business of just grubbing for a living was not good enough. Life was menial and lacked enchantment. I grew melancholy and dissatisfied and took lonely walks on Sunday and listened to park bands. I could support neither my own company nor that of anyone else. And of course, the obvious thing happened: I fell in love.

We were playing at the Streatham Empire. In those days we performed at two or three music halls nightly, travelling from one to the other in a private bus. At Streatham we were on early in order to appear later at the Canterbury Music Hall and then the Tivoli. It was daylight when we started work. The heat was oppressive and the Streatham Empire was half empty, which, incidentally, did not detract from my melancholy.

A song-and-dance troupe preceded us called 'Bert Coutts' Yankee-Doodle Girls'. I was hardly aware of them. But the second evening, while I stood in the wings indifferent and apathetic, one of the girls slipped during the dance and the others began to giggle. One looked off and caught my eye to see if I were also enjoying the joke. I was suddenly held by two large brown eyes sparkling mischievously, belonging to a slim gazelle with a shapely oval face, a bewitching full mouth, and beautiful teeth—the effect was electric. When she came off, she asked me to hold a small mirror while she arranged her hair. This gave me a chance to scrutinise her. That was the beginning. By

Wednesday I had asked her if I could meet her on Sunday. She laughed. 'I don't even know what you look like without the red nose!'—I was playing the comedy drunk in *Mumming Birds*, dressed in long tails and a white tie.

'My nose is not quite this red, I hope, and I'm not quite as decrepit as I look,' I said, 'and to prove it I'll bring a photo of myself tomorrow night.'

I gave her what I thought was a flattering one of a sad, callow youth, wearing a black stock tie.

'Oh, but you're quite young,' she said. 'I thought you were much older.'

'How old did you think I was?'

'At least thirty.'

I smiled. 'I'm going on for nineteen.'

As we were rehearsing every day, it was impossible to meet her during the week. However, she promised to meet me at Kennington Gate at four o'clock on Sunday afternoon.

Sunday was a perfect summer's day and the sun shone continuously. I wore a dark suit that was cut smartly in at the waist, also a dark stock tie, and sported a black ebony cane. It was ten minutes to four, and I was all nerves, waiting and watching passengers alighting from tram-cars.

As I waited I realised I had not seen her without make-up. I began to lose the vision of what she looked like. Much as I tried, I could not recall her features. A mild fear seized me. Perhaps her beauty was bogus! An illusion! Every ordinary-looking young girl that alighted sent me into throes of despair. Would I be disappointed? Had I been duped by my own imagination or by the artifices of theatrical make-up?

At three minutes to four, someone got off a tram-car and came towards me. My heart sank. Her looks were disappointing. The depressing thought of facing the whole afternoon with her, keeping up a pretence of enthusiasm, was already deplorable. However, I raised my hat and beamed; she stared indignantly and passed on. Thank God it was not she.

Then precisely at one minute past four, a young girl alighted from a tram-car, came forward and stopped before me. She was without make-up and looked more beautiful than ever, wearing a simple sailor hat, a blue reefer coat with brass buttons, with her hands dug deep in her overcoat pockets. 'Here I am,' she said.

Her presence so overwhelmed me that I could hardly talk. I became agitated. I could think of nothing to say or do. 'Let's take a taxi,' I said huskily, looking up and down the road, then turned to her. 'Where would you like to go?'

She shrugged. 'Anywhere.'

'Then let's go over to the West End for dinner.'

'I've had dinner,' she said calmly.

'We'll discuss it in the taxi,' I said.

The intensity of my emotion must have bewildered her, for all during the drive I kept repeating: 'I know I'm going to regret this—you're too beautiful!' I tried vainly to be amusing and impress her. I had drawn three pounds from the bank and had planned to take her to the Trocadero, where, in an atmosphere of music and plush elegance, she could see me under the most romantic auspices. I wanted to sweep her off her feet. But she remained cool-eyed and somewhat perplexed at my utterances, one in particular: that she was my Nemesis, a word I had recently acquired.

How little she understood what it all meant to me. It had little to do with sex; more important was her association. To meet elegance and beauty in my station of life was rare.

That evening at the Trocadero, I tried to persuade her to have dinner, but to no avail. She would have a sandwich to keep me company, she said. As we were occupying a whole table in a very posh restaurant, I felt it incumbent to order an elaborate meal which I really did not want. The dinner was a solemn ordeal: I was uncertain which implement to eat with. I bluffed through the meal with a *dégagé* charm, even to my casualness in using the finger-bowl, but I think we were both happy to leave the restaurant and relax.

After the Trocadero she decided to go home. I suggested a taxi, but she preferred to walk. As she lived in Camberwell nothing suited me better; it meant I could spend more time with her.

Now that my emotions had simmered down she seemed more at ease. That evening we walked along the Thames Embankment, Hetty chattering away about her girl friends, pleasantries and other inconsequential things. But I was hardly aware of what she was saying. I only knew that the night was ecstatic—that I was walking in Paradise with inner blissful excitement.

After I left her I returned to the Embankment, possessed! And illumined with kindly light and a fervent goodwill, I distributed among the derelicts who slept on the Thames Embankment the remainder of my three pounds.

We promised to meet the following morning at seven o'clock because she had rehearsals at eight o'clock somewhere in Shaftesbury Avenue. It was a walk of about a mile and a half from her house to the Underground in the Westminster Bridge Road, and although I worked late, never getting to bed before two o'clock, I was up at dawn to meet her.

Camberwell Road was now touched with magic because Hetty Kelly lived there. Those morning walks with hands clasped all the way to the Underground were bliss mingled with confused longings. Shabby, depressing Camberwell Road, which I used to avoid, now had lure as I walked in its morning mist, thrilled at Hetty's outline in the distance coming towards me. During those walks I never remembered anything she said. I was too enthralled, believing that a mystic force had brought us together and that our union was an affinity predetermined by fate.

Three mornings I had known her; three abbreviated little mornings which made the rest of the day non-existent, until the next morning. But on the fourth morning her manner changed.

She met me coldly, without enthusiasm, and would not take my hand. I reproached her for it and jokingly accused her of not being in love with me.

'You expect too much,' she said. 'After all I am only fifteen and you are four years older than I am."

I would not assimilate the sense of her remark. But I could not ignore the distance she had suddenly placed between us. She was looking straight ahead, walking elegantly with a schoolgirl stride, both hands dug in her overcoat pockets.

'In other words, you really don't love me,' I said.

'I don't know,' she answered.

I was stunned. 'If you don't know, then you don't.' For answer, she walked in silence. 'You see what a prophet I am,' I continued lightly. 'I told you I would regret ever having met you.'

I tried to search her mind and find out to what extent her feeling was for me, and to all my questions she kept replying: 'I don't know.'

'Would you marry me?' I challenged.

'I'm too young.'

'Well, if you were compelled to marry would it be me or someone else?'

But she was non-committal and kept repeating: 'I don't know . . . I like you . . . but——'

'But you don't love me,' I interposed with a sinking feeling.

She was silent. It was a cloudy morning and the streets looked drab and depressing.

'The trouble is I have let this thing go too far,' I said huskily. We had reached the entrance to the Underground. 'I think we'd better part and never see each other again,' I said, wondering what would be her reaction.

She looked solemn.

I took her hand and patted it tenderly. 'Goodbye, it's better this way. Already you have too much of a power over me.'

'Goodbye,' she answered. 'I'm sorry.'

The apology struck me as deadly. And as she disappeared into the Underground, I felt an unbearable emptiness.

What had I done? Was I too rash? I should not have challenged her. I'd been a pompous idiot and made it impossible to see her again—unless I made myself ridiculous. What was I to do? I could only suffer. If only I could submerge this mental agony in sleep until I meet her again. At all costs I must keep away from her until she wants to see me. Perhaps I was too serious, too intense. The next time we meet I shall be levitous and detached. But will she want to see me again? Surely she must! She cannot dismiss me so easily.

The next morning I could not resist walking up the Camberwell Road. I did not meet her, but met her mother. 'What have you done to Hetty!' she said. 'She came home crying and said you never wanted to see her again.'

I shrugged and smiled ironically. 'What has she done to me?' Then hesitantly I asked if I could see her again.

She shook her head warily. 'No, I don't think you should.'

I invited her to have a drink, so we went to a corner pub to talk it over, and after I entreated her to let me see Hetty again she consented.

When we reached the house, Hetty opened the door. She was surprised and concerned when she saw me. She had just washed her face with Sunlight soap—it smelt so fresh. She remained standing at the front door, her large eyes looking cold and objective. I could see it was hopeless.

'Well,' I said, attempting to be humorous, 'I've come to say goodbye again.'

She didn't answer, but I could see she was anxious to be rid of me.

I extended my hand and smiled. 'So goodbye again,' I said.

'Goodbye,' she answered coldly.

I turned and heard the street door gently closing behind me.

Although I had met her but five times, and scarcely any of our meetings lasted longer than twenty minutes, that brief encounter affected me for a long time.

VII

In 1909 I went to Paris. Monsieur Burnell of the Folies Bergère had engaged the Karno Company to play for a limited engagement of one month. How excited I was at the thought of going to a foreign country! The week before sailing we played at Woolwich, a dank, miserable week in a miserable town, and I looked forward to the change. We were to leave early Sunday morning. I almost missed the train, running down the platform and catching the last luggage van, in which I rode all the way to Dover. I had a genius for missing trains in those days.

The rain came down in torrents over the Channel, but the first sight of France through the mist was an unforgettable thrill. 'It isn't England,' I had to keep reminding myself, 'it's the Continent! France!' It had always appealed to my imagination. My father was part French, in fact the Chaplin family originally came from France. They landed in England in the time of the Huguenots. Father's uncle would say with pride that a French general established the English branch of the Chaplin family.

It was late autumn and the journey from Calais to Paris was dreary. Nevertheless, as we neared Paris my excitement grew. We had passed through bleak, lonely country. Then gradually out of the darkened sky we saw an illumination. 'That,' said a Frenchman in the carriage with us, 'is the reflection of Paris.'

Paris was everything I expected. The drive from the Gare du Nord to the rue Geoffroy-Marie had me excited and impatient; I wanted to stop at every corner and walk. It was seven in the evening; the golden lights shone invitingly from the cafés and their outside tables spoke of an enjoyment of life. But for the innovation of a few motor-cars, it was still the Paris of Monet, Pissarro and Renoir. It was Sunday and everyone seemed pleasure-bent. Gaiety and vitality were in the air. Even my room in the rue Geoffroy-Marie, with its stone floor, which I called

19. Karno's Company hockey team. I am seated second from the left.
Stan Laurel is standing behind me.

Arcadia Skating Rink
LEVENSHULME.

A GRAND

HOCKEY MATCH

Will be played at the above Rink

On Saturday Afternoon, April 2nd,
BULLY OFF AT 4 P.M.

ARCADIA
VERSUS

Fred Karno's Team
(From the Kings Theatre, Longsight).

FRED KARNO'S TEAM:
Goal: Ernie Stone; Full Back: Jimmy Berrisford;
Forwards: Fred Jordan, Ted Banks (Capt.),
and Charlie Chaplin.
Manager   -   -   Frank O'Niel.

ARCADIA TEAM:
Goal: J. Taylor; Back: E. Stanion;
Forwards: Birchall, Beattie, and Standfast.

S. SHUTES, Trade Union Printer, Levenshulme.

20. Announcing a match against Arcadia

21. With Alf Reeves, his wife and Muriel Palmer on our way
to America for the Karno Company

22. Before my success

23. . . . and after

my Bastille, could not dampen my ardour, for one lived sitting at tables outside bistros and cafés.

Sunday night was free, so we could see the show at the Folies Bergère, where we were to open the following Monday. No theatre, I thought, ever exuded such glamour, with its gilt and plush, its mirrors and large crystal chandeliers. In the thick-carpeted foyers and dress circle the world promenaded. Be-jewelled Indian princes with pink turbans and French and Turkish officers with plumed helmets sipped cognac at liqueur bars. In the large outer foyer music played as ladies checked their wraps and fur coats, baring their white shoulders. They were the habituées who discreetly solicited and promenaded the foyers and the dress circle. In those days they were beautiful and courtly.

The Folies Bergère also had professional linguists who strolled about the theatre with the word 'Interpreter' on their caps, and I made a friend of the head one, who could speak several languages fluently.

After our performance I would wear my stage evening-dress clothes and mingle with the promenaders. One gracile creature with a swan-like neck and white skin made my heart flutter. She was a tall Gibson Girl type, extremely beautiful, with retroussé nose and long dark eye-lashes, and wore a black velvet dress with long white gloves. As she went up the dress-circle stairs, she dropped a glove. Quickly I picked it up.

'*Merci*,' she said.

'I wish you would drop it again,' I said mischievously.

'*Pardon?*'

Then I realised she did not understand English and I spoke no French. So I went to my friend the interpreter. 'There's a dame that arouses my concupiscence. But she looks very ex-pensive.'

He shrugged. 'Not more than a louis.'

'Good,' I said, although a louis in those days was a lot, I thought—and it was.

I had the interpreter put down a few French *phrases d'amour* on the back of a postcard: '*Je vous adore*', '*Je vous ai aimée la première fois que je vous ai vue*', etc., which I intended to use at the propitious moment. I asked him to make the preliminary arrangements and he acted as courier, going from one to the other. Eventually he came back and said: 'It's all settled, one louis, but you must pay her cab-fare to her apartment and back.'

I temporised a moment. 'Where does she live?' I asked.

'It won't cost more than ten francs.'

Ten francs was disastrous, as I had not anticipated that extra charge. 'Couldn't she walk?' I said, jokingly.

'Listeñ, this girl is first-class, you must pay her fare,' he said. So I acquiesced.

After the arrangements had been settled, I passed her on the dress-circle stairs. She smiled and I glanced back at her. '*Ce soir!*'

'*Enchantée, monsieur!*'

As we were on before the interval I promised to meet her after my performance. Said my friend: 'You hail a cab while I get the girl, then you won't waste time.'

'Waste time?'

As we drove along the Boulevard des Italiens, the lights and shadows passing over her face and long white neck, she looked ravishing. I glanced surreptitiously at my French on the postcard. '*Je vous adore*,' I began.

She laughed, showing her perfect white teeth. 'You speak very well French.'

'*Je vous ai aimée la première fois que je vous ai vue*,' I continued emotionally.

She laughed again and corrected my French, explaining that I should use the familiar '*tu*'. She thought about it and laughed again. She looked at her watch, but it had stopped; she indicated she wanted to know the time, explaining that at twelve o'clock she had a very important appointment.

'Not this evening,' I said coyly.

'*Oui, ce soir.*'

'But you're fully engaged this evening, *toute la nuit!*'

She suddenly looked startled. '*Oh, non, non, non! Pas toute la nuit!*'

Then it became sordid. '*Vingt francs pour le moment?*'

'*C'est ça!*' she replied emphatically.

'I'm sorry,' I said, 'I think I'd better stop the cab.'

And after paying the driver to take her back to the Folies Bergère, I got out, a very sad and disillusioned young man.

We could have stayed at the Folies Bergère ten weeks, as we were a great success, but Mr Karno had other bookings. My salary was six pounds a week, and I spent every penny of it. A cousin of my brother's, related to Sydney's father in some way, made himself known to me. He was rich and belonged to the so-called upper class, and during his stay in Paris he showed me a very good time. He was stage-struck and even went so far as having his moustache shaved off in order to pass as a member of our company, so that he could be allowed back stage. Unfortunately, he had to return to England, where, I understand, he was hauled over the coals by his august parents and sent to South America.

Before going to Paris, I had heard that Hetty's troupe were playing at the Folies Bergère, so I was all set to meet her again. The night I arrived I went back stage and made enquiries, but I learnt from one of the ballet girls that the troupe had left a week previously for Moscow. While I was talking to the girl a harsh voice came over the stairs:

'Come here at once! How dare you talk to strangers!'

It was the girl's mother. I tried to explain that I merely wanted information about a friend of mine, but the mother ignored me. 'Never mind talking to that man, come up here at once.'

I was annoyed at her crassness. Later, however, I became better acquainted with her. She lived in the same hotel as I did with her two daughters, who were members of the

Folies Bergère ballet. The younger, thirteen, was the *première danseuse*, very pretty and talented, but the older one, fifteen, had neither talent nor looks. The mother was French, buxom and about forty, married to a Scotsman who was living in England. After we opened at the Folies Bergère, she came to me and apologised for being so abrupt. That was the beginning of a very friendly relationship. I was continually invited to their rooms for tea, which they made in their bedroom.

When I think back, I was incredibly innocent. One afternoon when the children were out and Mama and I were alone her attitude became strange and she began to tremble as she poured the tea. I had been talking about my hopes and dreams, my loves and disappointments, and she became quite moved. As I got up to put my tea-cup on the table, she came over to me.

'You are sweet,' she said, cupping my face with her hands and looking intensely into my eyes. 'Such a nice boy as you should not be hurt.' Her gaze became inverse, strange and hypnotic, and her voice trembled. 'Do you know, I love you like a son,' she said, still holding my face in her hands. Then slowly her face came to mine, and she kissed me.

'Thank you,' I said, sincerely—and innocently kissed her back. She continued transfixing me with her gaze, her lips trembling and her eyes glazed, then, suddenly checking herself, she went about pouring a fresh cup of tea. Her manner had changed and a certain humour played about her mouth. 'You are very sweet,' she said, 'I like you very much.'

She confided in me about her daughters. 'The young one is a very good girl,' she said, 'but the older must be watched; she is becoming a problem.'

After the show she would invite me to supper in her large bedroom in which she and her younger daughter slept, and before returning to my room I would kiss the mother and her younger daughter good-night; I would then have to go through a small room where the elder daughter slept. One night as I was passing through the room, she beckoned to me and whispered: 'Leave your door open and I will come up when the family is asleep.' Believe it or not, I threw her back on her bed indignantly and stalked out of the room. At the end of their engagement at the Folies Bergère, I heard that the elder daughter, still in her fifteenth year, had run off with a dog-trainer, a heavy-set German of sixty.

But I was not as innocent as I appeared. Members of the troupe and I occasionally spent a night carousing through the bordels and doing all the hoydenish things that youth will do. One night, after drinking several absinthes, I got into a fight with an ex-lightweight prize-fighter named Ernie Stone. It started in a restaurant, and after the waiters and the police had separated us he said: 'I'll see you at the hotel,' where we were both staying. He had the room above me, and at four in the morning I rolled home and knocked at his door.

'Come in,' he said briskly, 'and take off your shoes so we won't make a noise.'

Quietly we stripped to the waist, then faced each other. We hit and ducked for what seemed an interminable length of time. Several times he hit me square on the chin, but to no effect. 'I thought you could punch,' I sneered. He made a lunge, missed and smashed his head against the wall, almost knocking himself out. I tried to finish him off, but my punches were weak. I could hit him with impunity, but I had no strength behind my punch. Suddenly, I received a blow full in the mouth which shook my front teeth, and that sobered me up. 'Enough,' I said, 'I don't want to lose my teeth.' He came over and embraced me, then looked in the mirror: I had cut his face to ribbons. My hands were swollen like boxing gloves, and blood was on the ceiling, on the curtains and on the walls. How it got there, I do not know.

During the night the blood trickled down the side of my mouth and across my neck. The little *première danseuse*, who used to bring me up a cup of tea in the morning, screamed, thinking I had committed suicide. And I have never fought anyone since.

One night the interpreter came to me saying that a celebrated musician wanted to meet me, and would I go to his box? The invitation was mildly interesting, for in the box with him was a most beautiful, exotic lady, a member of the Russian Ballet. The interpreter introduced me. The gentleman said that he had enjoyed my performance and was surprised to see how young I was. At these compliments I bowed politely, occasionally taking a furtive glance at his friend. 'You are instinctively a musician and a dancer,' said he.

Feeling there was no reply to this compliment other than to smile sweetly, I glanced at the interpreter and bowed politely. The musician stood up and extended his hand and I stood up. 'Yes,' he said, shaking my hand, 'you are a true artist.' After we left I turned to the interpreter: 'Who was the lady with him?'

'She is a Russian ballet dancer, Mademoiselle ——' It was a very long and difficult name.

'And what was the gentleman's name?' I asked.

'Debussy,' he answered, 'the celebrated composer.'

'Never heard of him,' I remarked.

It was the year of the famous scandal and trial of Madame Steinheil, who was tried and found not guilty of murdering her husband; the year of the sensational 'pom-pom' dance that showed couples indecently rotating together in a libidinous display; the year incredible tax laws were passed of sixpence in the pound on personal income; the year Debussy introduced his *Prélude à l'Après-midi d'un Faune* to England, where it was booed and the audience walked out.

*   *   *

With sadness I returned to England and began a tour of the provinces. What a contrast to Paris! Those mournful Sunday evenings in northern towns: everything closed, and the doleful clang of reprimanding bells that accompanied carousing youths and giggling wenches parading the darkened high streets and back alleys. It was their only Sunday evening diversion.

Six months had drifted by in England and I had settled down to my usual routine, when news came from the London office that made life more exciting. Mr Karno informed me that I was to take the place of Harry Weldon in the second season of *The Football Match*. Now I felt that my star was in the ascendant. This was my chance. Although I had made a success in *Mumming Birds* and other sketches in our repertoire, those were minor achievements compared to playing the lead in *The Football Match*. Moreover, we were to open at the Oxford, the most important music hall in London. We were to be the main attraction and I was to have my name featured for the first time at the top of the bill. This was a considerable step up. If I were a success at the Oxford it would establish a kudos that would enable me to demand a large salary and eventually branch out with my own sketches, in fact it would lead to all sorts of wonderful schemes. As practically the same cast was engaged for *The Football Match*, we needed only a week's rehearsal. I had thought a great deal about how to play the part. Harry Weldon had a Lancashire accent. I decided to play it as a cockney.

But at the first rehearsal I had an attack of laryngitis. I did everything to save my voice, speaking in whispers, inhaling vapours and spraying my throat, until anxiety robbed me of all unctuousness and comedy for the part.

On the opening night, every vein and cord in my throat was strained to the utmost with a vengeance. But I could not be heard. Karno came round afterwards with an expression of mingled disappointment and contempt. 'No one could hear you,' he said reprovingly. I assured him that my voice would be better the next night, but it was not. In fact it was worse, for it had been forced to such a degree that I was in danger of losing it completely. The next night my understudy went on. As a consequence the engagement finished after the first week. All my hopes and dreams of that Oxford engagement had collapsed, and the disappointment of it laid me low with influenza.

*   *   *

I had not seen Hetty in over a year. In a state of weakness and melancholy after the 'flu, I thought of her again and wandered late one night towards her home in Camberwell. But the house was empty with a sign: 'To Let'.

I continued wandering the streets with no special objective. Suddenly out of the night a figure appeared, crossing the road and coming towards me.

'Charlie! What are you doing up this way?' It was Hetty. She was dressed in a black sealskin coat with a round sealskin hat.

'I came to meet you,' I said, jokingly.

She smiled. 'You're very thin.'

I told her I had just recovered from 'flu. She was seventeen now, quite pretty and smartly dressed.

'But the thing is, what are you doing up this way?' I asked.

'I've been visiting a friend and now I'm going to my brother's house. Would you like to come along?' she answered.

On the way, she told me that her sister had married an American millionaire, Frank J. Gould, and that they lived in Nice, and that she was leaving London in the morning to join them.

That evening I stood watching her dancing coquettishly with her brother. She was acting silly and siren-like with him, and in spite of myself I could not preclude a feeling that my ardour for her had slightly diminished. Had she become commonplace like any other girl? The thought saddened me, and I found myself looking at her objectively.

Her figure had developed, and I noticed the contours of her breasts and thought their protuberance small and not very alluring. Would I marry her even if I could afford to? No, I did not want to marry anyone.

As I walked home with her on that cold and brilliant night, I must have been sadly objective as I spoke about the possibility of her having a very wonderful and happy life. 'You sound so wistful, I could almost weep,' she said.

That night I went home feeling triumphant, for I had touched her with my sadness and had made my personality felt.

Karno put me back into *Mumming Birds* and, ironically, it was not more than a month before I completely recovered my voice. Great as my disappointment was about *The Football Match*, I tried not to dwell on it. But I was haunted by a thought that perhaps I was not equal to taking Weldon's place. And behind it all was the ghost of my failure at the Foresters'. As I had not fully retrieved my confidence, every new sketch in which I played the leading comedy part was a trial of fear. And now the alarming and a most resolute day came to notify Mr Karno that my contract had run out and that I wanted a raise.

Karno could be cynical and cruel to anyone he disliked. Because he liked me I had never seen that side of him, but he could indeed be most crushing in a vulgar way. During a performance of one of his comedies, if he did not like a comedian, he would stand in the wings and hold his nose and give an audible raspberry. But he did this once too often and the comedian left the stage and lunged at him; that was the last time he resorted to such vulgar measures. And now I stood confronting him about a new contract.

'Well,' he said, smiling cynically, 'you want a raise and the theatre circuits want a cut.' He shrugged. 'Since the fiasco at the Oxford Music Hall, we've had nothing but complaints. They say the company's not up to the mark—a scratch crowd.'*

'Well, they can hardly blame me for that,' I said.

'But they do,' he answered, pinning me with a steady gaze.

'What do they complain about?' I asked.

* In the Karno troupe it took at least six months working together before we could perfect a tempo. Until then it was called a 'scratch crowd'.

He cleared his throat and looked at the floor. 'They say you're not competent.'

Although the remark hit me in the pit of the stomach, it also infuriated me, but I replied calmly: 'Well, other people don't think so, and they're willing to give me more than I'm getting here.' This was not true—I had no other offer.

'They say the show is awful and the comedian's no good. Here,' he said, picking up the phone, 'I'll call up the Star, Bermondsey, and you can hear for yourself... I understand you did poor business last week,' he said over the phone.

'Lousy!' came a voice.

Karno grinned. 'How do you account for it?'

'A dud show!'

'What about Chaplin, the principal comedian? Wasn't he any good?'

'He stinks!' said the voice.

Karno offered me the phone and grinned. 'Listen for yourself.'

I took the phone. 'Maybe he stinks, but not half as much as your stink-pot theatre!' I said.

Karno's attempt to cut me down was not a success. I told him that if he also felt that way there was no need to renew my contract. Karno in many ways was a shrewd man, but he was not a psychologist. Even if I did stink it wasn't good business of Karno to have a man at the other end of the phone tell me so. I was getting five pounds and, although my confidence was low, I demanded six. To my surprise Karno gave it to me, and again I entered his good graces.

*   *   *

Alf Reeves, the manager of Karno's American company, returned to England and rumour had it that he was looking for a principal comedian to take back with him to the States.

Since my major setback at the Oxford Music Hall, I was full of the idea of going to America, not alone for the thrill and

122

adventure of it, but because it would mean renewed hope, a new beginning in a new world. Fortunately *Skating*, one of our new sketches in which I was the leading comedian, was going over with great success in Birmingham and when Mr Reeves joined our company there I pinned on as much charm as I could; with the result that Reeves wired Karno that he had found his comedian for the States. But Karno had other plans for me. This sickening fact left me in doubt for several weeks until he became interested in a sketch called *The Wow-wows*. It was a burlesque on initiating a member into a secret society. Reeves and I thought the show silly, fatuous and without merit. But Karno was obsessed with the idea and insisted that America was full of secret societies and that a burlesque on them would be a great success there, so to my happy relief and excitement, Karno chose me to play the principal part in *The Wow-wows* for America.

This chance to go to the United States was what I needed. In England I felt I had reached the limit of my prospects; besides, my opportunities there were circumscribed. With scant educational background, if I failed as a music-hall comedian I would have little chance but to do menial work. In the States the prospects were brighter.

The night before sailing, I walked about the West End of London, pausing at Leicester Square, Coventry Street, the Mall and Piccadilly, with the wistful feeling that it would be the last time I would see London, for I had made up my mind to settle permanently in America. I walked until two in the morning, wallowing in the poetry of deserted streets and my own sadness.

I loathed saying goodbye. Whatever one feels about parting from relations and friends, to be seen off by them only rubs it in. I was up at six in the morning. Therefore, I did not bother to wake Sydney, but left a note on the table stating: 'Off to America. Will keep you posted. Love, Charlie.'

VIII

WE were twelve days on the high seas in terrible weather, bound for Quebec. For three days we lay to with a broken rudder. Nevertheless, my heart was light and gay at the thought of going to another land. We travelled via Canada on a cattle boat, and although there were no cattle aboard there were plenty of rats and they perched arrogantly at the foot of my bunk until I threw a shoe at them.

It was the beginning of September and we passed Newfoundland in a fog. At last we sighted the mainland. It was a drizzling day, and the banks of the St Lawrence River looked desolate. Quebec from the boat looked like the ramparts where Hamlet's ghost might have walked, and I began to wonder about the States.

But as we travelled on to Toronto, the country became increasingly beautiful in autumnal colours and I became more hopeful. In Toronto we changed trains and went through the American Immigration. At ten o'clock on a Sunday morning we at last arrived in New York. When we got off the street-car at Times Square, it was somewhat of a let-down. Newspapers were blowing about the road and pavement, and Broadway looked seedy, like a slovenly woman just out of bed. On almost every street corner there were elevated chairs with shoe-lasts sticking up and people sitting comfortably in shirt-sleeves getting their shoes shined. They gave one the impression of finishing their toilet on the street. Many looked like strangers, standing aimlessly about the sidewalks as if they had just left the railroad station and were filling in time between trains.

However, this was New York, adventurous, bewildering, a little frightening. Paris, on the other hand, had been friendlier. Even though I could not speak the language, Paris had welcomed me on every street corner with its bistros and outside cafés. But New York was essentially a place of big business.

The tall skyscrapers seemed ruthlessly arrogant and to care little for the convenience of ordinary people; even the saloon bars had no place for the customers to sit, only a long brass rail to rest a foot on, and the popular eating places, though clean and done in white marble, looked cold and clinical.

I took a back room in one of the brownstone houses off Forty-third Street, where the Times Building now stands. It was dismal and dirty and made me homesick for London and our little flat. In the basement was a cleaning and pressing establishment and during the week the fetid odour of clothes being pressed and steamed wafted up and added to my discomfort.

That first day I felt quite inadequate. It was an ordeal to go into a restaurant and order something because of my English accent—and the fact that I spoke slowly. So many spoke in a rapid, clipped way that I felt uncomfortable for fear I might stutter and waste their time.

I was alien to this slick tempo. In New York even the owner of the smallest enterprise acts with alacrity. The shoe-black flips his polishing rag with alacrity, the bartender serves a beer with alacrity, sliding it up to you along the polished surface of the bar. The soda clerk, when serving an egg malted milk, performs like a hopped-up juggler. In a fury of speed he snatches up a glass, attacking everything he puts into it, vanilla flavour, blob of ice-cream, two spoonfuls of malt, a raw egg which he deposits with one crack, then adding milk, all of which he shakes in a container and delivers in less than a minute.

On the Avenue that first day many looked as I felt, lone and isolated; others swaggered along as though they owned the place. The behaviour of many people seemed dour and metallic as if to be agreeable or polite would prove a weakness. But in the evening as I walked along Broadway with the crowd dressed in their summer clothes, I became reassured. We had left England in the middle of a bitter cold September and arrived in New York in an Indian summer with a temperature of eighty degrees; and as I walked along Broadway it began to light up with myriads of coloured electric bulbs and sparkled like a brilliant jewel. And in the warm night my attitude changed and the meaning of America came to me: the tall skyscrapers, the brilliant, gay lights, the thrilling display of advertisements stirred me with hope and a sense of adventure. 'This is it!' I said to myself. 'This is where I belong!'

Everyone on Broadway seemed to be in show business; actors, vaudevillians, circus performers and entertainers were everywhere, on the street, in restaurants, hotels and department stores, all talking shop. One heard names of theatre-owners, Lee Shubert, Martin Beck, William Morris, Percy Williams, Klaw and Erlanger, Frohman, Sullivan and Considine, Pantages. Whether charwoman, elevator boy, waiter, street-car conductor, barman, milkman or baker, they all talked like showmen. One heard snatches of conversation in the streets, motherly old women, looking like farmers' wives, saying: 'He's just finished three a day out West for Pantages.* With the right material that boy should make big-time vaudeville.' 'Did you catch Al Jolson at the Winter Garden?' says a janitor. 'He certainly saved the show for Jake.'

Newspapers each day devoted a whole page to theatre, got up like a racing chart, indicating vaudeville acts coming in first, second and third in popularity and applause, like race-horses. We had not entered the race yet and I was anxious to know in what position we would finish on the chart. We were to play the Percy Williams circuit for six weeks only. After that we had no further bookings. On the result of that engagement depended the length of our stay in America. If we failed, we would return to England.

We took a rehearsal room and had a week of rehearsing *The Wow-wows*. In the cast was old Whimsical Walker, the famous Drury Lane clown. He was over seventy, with a deep, resonant

*Pantages circuit, which gave three shows a day.

voice, but had no diction, as we discovered at rehearsals, and he had the major part of explaining the plot. Such a line as 'The fun will be furious, ad libitum', he could not say and never did. The first night he spluttered: 'Ablib-blum', and eventually it became 'ablibum', but never the correct word.

In America, Karno had a great reputation. We were, therefore, the headline attraction over a programme of excellent artists. And although I hated the sketch, I naturally tried to make the best of it. I was hopeful that it might be what Karno called 'the very thing for America'.

I will not describe the nerves, agony and suspense that preceded my entrance the first night, or my embarrassment as the American artists stood in the wings watching us. My first joke was considered a big laugh in England and a barometer for how the rest of the comedy would go over. It was a camping scene. I entered from a tent with a tea-cup.

ARCHIE (me): Good morning, Hudson. Do you mind giving me a little water?
HUDSON: Certainly. What do you want it for?
ARCHIE: I want to take a bath.
(A faint snicker, then cold silence from the audience.)
HUDSON: How did you sleep last night, Archie?
ARCHIE: Oh, terribly. I dreamt I was being chased by a caterpillar.

Still deadly silence. And so we droned on, with the faces of the Americans in the wings growing longer and longer. But they were gone before we had finished our act.

It was a silly, dull sketch and I had advised Karno not to open with it. We had other much funnier sketches in our repertoire, such as *Skating*, *The Dandy Thieves*, *The Post Office* and *Mr Perkins, M.P.*, which would have been amusing to an American audience. But Karno was stubborn.

To say the least, failure in a foreign country is distressing. Appearing each night before a cold and silent audience as they listened to our effusive, jovial English comedy was a grim affair. We entered and exited from the theatre like fugitives. For six weeks we endured this ignominy. The other performers quarantined us as if we had the plague. When we gathered in the wings to go on, crushed and humiliated, it was as though we were about to be lined up and shot.

Although I felt lonely and rejected, I was thankful to be living alone. At least I had not to share my humiliation with others. During the day I walked interminably through long avenues that seemed to lead to nowhere, interesting myself in visiting zoos, parks, aquariums and museums. Since our failure, New York now seemed too formidable, its buildings too high, its competitive atmosphere overpowering. Those magnificent houses on Fifth Avenue were not homes but monuments of success. Its opulent towering buildings and fashionable shops seemed a ruthless reminder of how inadequate I was.

I took long walks across the city towards the slum district, passing through the park in Madison Square, where derelict old gargoyles sat on benches in a despairing stupor, staring at their feet. Then I moved on to Third and Second Avenues. Here poverty was callous, bitter and cynical, a sprawling, yelling, laughing, crying poverty piling around doorways, on fire escapes and spewing about the streets. It was all very depressing and made me want to hurry back to Broadway.

The American is an optimist preoccupied with hustling dreams, an indefatigable tryer. He hopes to make a quick 'killing'. Hit the jackpot! Get out from under! Sell out! Make the dough and run! Get into another racket! Yet this immoderate attitude began to brighten my spirit. Paradoxically enough, as a result of our failure I began to feel light and unhampered. There were many other opportunities in America. Why should I stick to show business? I was not dedicated to art. Get into another racket! I began to regain confidence. Whatever happened I was determined to stay in America.

As a distraction from failure I wanted to improve my

24. *The Wow-wows* opened at
the Colonial Theatre, New York,
on 3 October 1910

25. I was still playing the drunk in
A Night in a London Club two years
later

26. My manager, Alf Reeves

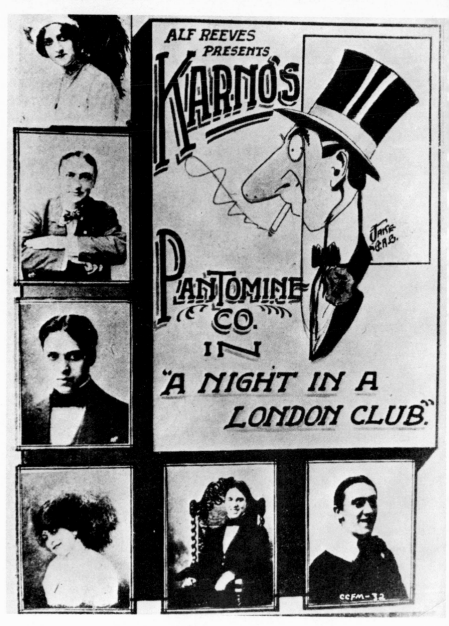

27. Amy Minister (top left), who married Alf Reeves (below her),
Muriel Palmer (bottom left) and Mike Asher (bottom right)

mind and educate myself; so I began browsing around the second-hand bookshops. I bought several text-books—Kellogg's *Rhetoric*, an English grammar and a Latin-English dictionary—with a determination to study them. But my resolutions went awry. No sooner had I looked at them than I packed them in the bottom of my trunk and forgot them—and not until our second visit to the States did I look at them again.

On the bill the first week in New York was an act called *Gus Edwards' School Days*, composed of children. In this troupe was a rather attractive scallywag who looked small for his sophisticated manner. He had a mania for gambling with cigarette coupons, which could be exchanged at the United Cigar Stores for items from a nickel-plated coffee-pot up to a grand piano; he was ready to shoot dice for them with stage-hands or anyone. He was an extraordinarily fast talker, by the name of Walter Winchell and though he never lost his rapid-fire talk, in later years his accuracy in reporting the truth often misfired.

Although our show was a failure, I personally got very good notices. Mike Simes of *Variety* said of me: 'There was at least one funny Englishman in the troupe and he will do for America.'

By now we had resigned ourselves to pack up and return to England after six weeks. But the third week we played at the Fifth Avenue Theatre, to an audience composed largely of English butlers and valets. To my surprise on the opening Monday night we went over with a bang. They laughed at every joke. Everyone in the company was surprised including myself, for I had expected the usual indifferent reception. In giving a perfunctory performance, I suppose I was relaxed. Consequently I could do no wrong.

During the week an agent saw us and booked us for a twenty-week tour out West on the Sullivan and Considine circuit. It was cheap vaudeville and we had to give three shows a day.

Although on that Sullivan and Considine first tour we were not a roaring success, we passed muster by comparison with the other acts. In those days the Middle West had charm. The tempo was slower, and the atmosphere was romantic; every drug-store and saloon had a dice-throwing desk in the entrance where one gambled for whatever products they sold. On Sunday morning Main Street was a continual hollow sound of rattling dice, which was pleasant and friendly; and many a time I won a dollar's worth of goods for ten cents.

Living was cheap. At a small hotel one could get a room and board for seven dollars a week, with three meals a day. Food was remarkably cheap. The saloon free-lunch counter was the mainstay of our troupe. For a nickel one could get a glass of beer änd the pick of a whole delicatessen counter. There were pigs' knuckles, sliced ham, potato salad, sardines, macaroni cheese, a variety of sliced sausages, liverwurst, salami and hot dogs. Some of our members took advantage of this and piled up their plates until the barman would intervene: 'Hey! Where the hell are you tracking with that load—to the Klondike?'

There were fifteen or more in our troupe and yet every member saved at least half of his wages, even after paying his own sleeping berth on the train. My salary was seventy-five dollars a week and fifty of it went regularly and resolutely into the Bank of Manhattan.

The tour took us to the Coast. Travelling with us out West on the same vaudeville bill was a handsome young Texan, a trapeze performer who could not make up his mind whether to continue with his partner on the trapeze or become a prize-fighter. Every morning I would put on the gloves with him, and, although he was taller and heavier than I was, I could hit him at will. We became very good friends, and after a boxing bout we would lunch together. His folks, he told me, were simple Texan farmers, and he would talk about life on the farm. Very soon we were talking ourselves into leaving show business and going into partnership, raising hogs.

Between us we had two thousand dollars and a dream of making a fortune; we planned to buy land for fifty cents an acre in Arkansas, two thousand acres to start with, and spend the rest buying hogs and improving the land. If all went well, we had it figured out that with the compound birth of hogs, averaging a litter of five a year, we could in five years make a hundred thousand dollars apiece.

Travelling on the train, we would look out of the window and see hog farms and go into paroxysms of excitement. We ate, slept and dreamed hogs. But for buying a book on scientific hog-raising I might have given up show business and become a hog-farmer, but that book, which graphically described the technique of castrating hogs, cooled my ardour and I soon forgot the enterprise.

On this tour I carried my violin and 'cello. Since the age of sixteen I had practised from four to six hours a day in my bedroom. Each week I took lessons from the theatre conductor or from someone he recommended. As I played left-handed, my violin was strung left-handed with the bass bar and sounding post reversed. I had great ambitions to be a concert artist, or, failing that, to use it in a vaudeville act, but as time went on I realised that I could never achieve excellence, so I gave it up.

In 1910 Chicago was attractive in its ugliness, grim and be-grimed, a city that still had the spirit of frontier days, a thriving, heroic metropolis of 'smoke and steel', as Carl Sandburg says. The vast flat plains approaching it are, I imagine, similar to the Russian steppes. It had a fierce pioneer gaiety that enlivened the senses, yet underlying it throbbed masculine loneliness. Counteracting this somatic ailment was a national distraction known as the burlesque show, consisting of a coterie of rough-and-tumble comedians supported by twenty or more chorus girls. Some were pretty, others shopworn. Some of the comedians were funny, most of the shows were smutty harem comedies—coarse and cynical affairs. The atmosphere was 'he-man', charged with profane sex antagonism which, para-doxically, insulated the audience from any normal sex desire —their reaction was to snivel at it. Chicago was full of these shows; one called *Watson's Beef Trust* had twenty enormously fat, middle-aged women displaying themselves in tights. Their combined weight went into tons, so it was advertised. Their photographs outside the theatre, showing them posing coyly, were sad and depressing.

In Chicago we lived up-town on Wabash Avenue in a small hotel; although grim and seedy, it had a romantic appeal, for most of the burlesque girls lived there. In each town we always made a bee-line for the hotel where the show girls stayed, with a libidinous hope that never materialised. The elevated trains swept by at night and flickered on my bedroom wall like an old-fashioned bioscope. Yet I loved that hotel, though nothing adventurous ever happened there.

One young girl, quiet and pretty, was for some reason always alone and walked with a self-conscious air. Occasionally I would pass her going in and out of the hotel lobby, but I never had the temerity to get acquainted, and I must say she gave me little encouragement.

When we left Chicago for the coast she was on the same train; burlesque companies going west usually toured the same route we were travelling and played in the same towns. Passing through the train, I saw her talking to a member of our company. Later he came and took his seat beside me. 'What sort of a girl is she?' I asked.

'Very sweet. Poor kid, I'm sorry for her.'

'Why?'

He leaned closer. 'Remember the rumour going around that one of the girls in the show had syphilis? Well, that's the one.'

In Seattle she was obliged to leave the company and enter a hospital. We made a collection for her, all the travelling companies contributing. Poor girl, everyone knew what was the matter with her. Nevertheless, she was thankful and two weeks later rejoined her company, cured by injections of Salvarsan, a new drug at that time.

In those days the red-light districts were rampant throughout

America. Chicago was especially noted for the House of All Nations, run by the Everly sisters, two middle-aged spinsters; it was notorious for having women of every nationality. Rooms were furnished in every style and décor: Turkish, Japanese, Louis XVI, even an Arab tent. It was the most elaborate establishment in the world, and the most expensive. Millionaires, industrial tycoons, cabinet ministers, senators and judges alike were its customers. Members of a convention usually terminated their concord by taking over the whole establishment for the evening. One wealthy sybarite was known to take up his abode there for three weeks without seeing daylight.

The further west we went the better I liked it. Looking out of the train at the vast stretches of wild land, though it was drear and sombre, filled me with promise. Space is good for the soul. It is broadening. My outlook was larger. Such cities as Cleveland, St Louis, Minneapolis, St Paul, Kansas City, Denver, Butte, Billings, throbbed with the dynamism of the future, and I was imbued with it.

We made many friends with the members of other vaudeville companies. In each town we would get together in the red-light district, six or more of us. Sometimes we won the affection of the madam of a bordel and she would close up the 'joint' for the night and we would take over. Occasionally some of the girls fell for the actors and would follow them to the next town.

The red-light district of Butte, Montana, consisted of a long street and several by-streets containing a hundred cribs in which young girls were installed ranging in age from sixteen up for one dollar. Butte boasted of having the prettiest women of any red-light district in the Middle West, and it was true. If one saw a pretty girl smartly dressed, one could rest assured she was from the red-light quarter doing her shopping. Off duty they looked neither right nor left and were most respectable. Years later I argued with Somerset Maugham about his Sadie Thompson character in the play *Rain*. Jeanne Eagels dressed her rather grotesquely, as I remember, with spring-side boots. I told him that no harlot in Butte, Montana, could make money if she dressed like that.

In 1910 Butte, Montana, was still a 'Nick Carter' town, with miners wearing top-boots and two-gallon hats and red neckerchiefs. I actually saw gun-play in the street, a fat old sheriff shooting at the heels of an escaped prisoner, who was eventually cornered in a blind alley without harm, fortunately.

My heart grew lighter as we travelled west: cities looked cleaner. Our route was Winnipeg, Tacoma, Seattle, Vancouver, Portland. In Winnipeg and Vancouver, audiences were essentially English and in spite of my pro-American leanings it was pleasant to play before them.

At last California!—a paradise of sunshine, orange groves, vineyards and palm-trees stretching along the Pacific coast for a thousand miles. San Francisco, the gateway to the Orient, was a city of good food and cheap prices; the first to introduce me to frogs' legs à la provençale, strawberry shortcake and avocado pears. We arrived in 1910, after the city had risen from the earthquake of 1906, or the fire, as they prefer to call it. There were still one or two cracks in the hilly streets, but little remnant of damage was left. Everything was new and bright, including my small hotel.

We played at the Empress, owned by Sid Grauman and his father, friendly, gregarious people. It was the first time I was featured alone on a poster with no mention of Karno. And the audience, what a delight! In spite of *The Wow-wows* being a dull show, there were packed houses every performance and screams of laughter. Grauman said enthusiastically: 'Any time you're through with the Karno outfit, come back here and we'll put on shows together.' This enthusiasm was new to me. In San Francisco one felt the spirit of optimism and enterprise.

Los Angeles, on the other hand, was an ugly city, hot and oppressive, and the people looked sallow and anaemic. It was a much warmer climate but had not the freshness of San

Francisco; nature has endowed the north of California with resources that will endure and flourish when Hollywood has disappeared into the prehistoric tar-pits of Wilshire Boulevard.

We finished our first tour in Salt Lake City, the home of the Mormons, which made me think of Moses leading the children of Israel. It is a gaping wide city, that seems to waver in the heat of the sun like a mirage, with wide streets that only a people who had traversed vast plains would conceive. Like the Mormons, the city is aloof and austere—and so was the audience.

After playing *The Wow-wows* on the Sullivan and Considine circuit, we came back to New York with the intention of returning directly to England, but Mr William Morris, who was fighting the other vaudeville trusts, gave us six weeks to play our whole repertoire at his theatre on Forty-second Street, New York City. We opened with *A Night in an English Music Hall*, which was a tremendous success.

During the week a young man and his friend had a late date with a couple of girls, so to kill time they wandered into William Morris's American Music Hall, where they happened to see our show. One remarked: 'If ever I become a big shot, there's a guy I'll sign up.' He was referring to my performance as the drunk in *A Night in an English Music Hall*. At the time he was working for D. W. Griffith as a movie extra in the Biograph Company, getting five dollars a day. He was Mack Sennett, who later formed the Keystone Film Company.

Having played a very successful six weeks' engagement for William Morris in New York, we were again booked for another twenty weeks' tour on the Sullivan and Considine circuit.

I felt sad as we drew near to the end of our second tour. There were three weeks more, San Francisco, San Diego, then Salt Lake City and back to England.

The day before leaving San Francisco, I took a stroll down Market Street and came upon a small shop with a curtained window and a sign reading: 'Your fortune told by hands and cards—one dollar.' I went in, slightly embarrassed, and was confronted by a plump woman of about forty who came from an inner room still chewing an interrupted meal. Perfunctorily she pointed to a small table against the wall facing the door, and without looking at me said: 'Sit down, please,' then she sat opposite. Her manner was abrupt. 'Shuffle these cards and cut them three times towards me, then lay the palms of your hands upwards on the table, please.' She turned the cards over and spread them, studied them, then looked at my hands. 'You're thinking about a long journey, which means you'll be leaving the States. But you return again shortly, and will enter a new business—something different from what you're doing at present.' Here she hesitated and became confused. 'Well, it's almost the same but it's different. I see tremendous success in this new venture; there's an extraordinary career ahead of you, but I don't know what it is.' For the first time she looked up at me, then took my hand. 'Oh yes, there's three marriages: the first two are not successful, but you end your life happily married with three children.' (She was wrong there!) Then she studied my hand again. 'Yes, you will make a tremendous fortune, it's a money-making hand.' Then she studied my face. 'You will die of bronchial pneumonia, at the age of eighty-two. A dollar, please. Is there any question you'd like to ask?'

'No,' I laughed, 'I think I'll leave well enough alone.'

In Salt Lake City, the newspapers were full of hold-ups and bank robberies. Customers in night-clubs and cafés were being lined up against the wall and robbed by masked bandits with stockings over their faces. There were three robberies in one night and they were terrorising the whole city.

After the show we usually went to a nearby saloon for a drink, occasionally getting acquainted with the customers. One evening a fat, jovial, round-faced man came in with two other men. The fat one, the oldest of the three, came over. 'Aren't you fellows playing the Empress in that English act?'

We nodded smilingly.

'I thought I recognised you! Hey, fellows! Come on over.'
He hailed his two companions and after introducing them asked
us to have a drink.

The fat one was an Englishman, although little trace of the
accent was left; a man about fifty, good-natured, with small
twinkling eyes and a florid face.

As the night wore on his two friends and members of
our company drifted away from us towards the bar, and I
found myself alone with 'Fat', as his young friends called
him.

He became confidential. 'I was back in the old country three
years ago,' he said, 'but it ain't the same—this here's the place.
Came here thirty years ago, a sucker, working my arse off in
them Montana copperfields—then I got wise to myself. "That's
a mug's game," I says. Now I've got chumps working for me.'
He pulled out an enormous wad of bills. 'Let's have another
drink.'

'Be careful,' I said, jokingly. 'You might get held up!'

He looked at me with a most evil, knowing smile, then
winked. 'Not this baby!'

A terrifying feeling came over me after that wink. It had
implied a great deal. He continued smiling, without taking his
eyes from me. 'Catch on?' he said.

I nodded wisely.

Then he spoke confidentially, bringing his face close to my
ear. 'See those two guys?' he whispered, referring to his friends.
'That's my outfit, two dumb clucks—no brains but plenty o'
guts.'

I put a finger to my lips cautiously, indicating that he might
be overheard.

'We're O.K., brother, we're shipping out tonight.' He continued: 'Listen, we're limeys, ain't we—from the old smoke?
I seen you at the Islington Empire many a time, falling in
and out of that box.' He grimaced. 'That's a tough racket,
brother.'

I laughed.

As he grew more confidential, he wanted to make a lifelong friend of me and to know my address in New York. 'I'll drop you a line just for old times' sake,' he said. Fortunately, I never heard from him again.

IX

I WAS not too upset at leaving the States, for I had made up my mind to return; how or when I did not know. Nevertheless, I looked forward to returning to London and our comfortable little flat. Since I had toured the States it had become a sort of shrine.

I had not heard from Sydney in a long time. His last letter stated that Grandfather was living in the flat. But on my arrival in London, Sydney met me at the station and told me that he had given up the flat, that he had married and was living in furnished rooms along the Brixton Road. This was a severe blow to me—to think that that cheerful little haven that had given substance to my sense of living, a pride in a home, was no more. . . . I was homeless. I rented a back room in the Brixton Road. It was so dismal that I resolved to return to the United States as soon as possible. That first night, London seemed as indifferent to my return as an empty slot machine when one had put a coin in it.

As Sydney was married and working every evening, I saw little of him; but on Sunday we both went to see Mother. It was a depressing day, for she was not well. She had just got over an obstreperous phase of singing hymns, and had been confined to a padded room. The nurse had warned us of this beforehand. Sydney saw her, but I had not the courage, so I waited. He came back upset, and said that she had been given shock treatment of icy cold showers and that her face was quite blue. This made us decide to put her into a private institution— we could afford it now—so we had her transferred to the same institution in which England's great comedian, the late Dan Leno, had been confined.

Each day I felt more of a nondescript and completely uprooted. I suppose had I returned to our little flat, my feelings might have been different. Naturally, gloom did not completely take over. Familiarity, custom and my kinship with England were deeply moving to me after arriving from the States. It was an ideal English summer and its romantic loveliness was unlike anything I had known elsewhere.

Mr Karno, the boss, invited me down to Tagg's Island for a week-end on his house-boat. It was rather an elaborate affair, with mahogany panelling and state-rooms for guests. At night it was lit up with festoons of coloured lights all round the boat, gay and charming, I thought. It was a beautiful warm evening, and after dinner we sat out on the upper deck under the coloured lights with our coffee and cigarettes. This was the England that could wean me away from any country.

Suddenly, a falsetto, foppish voice began screaming hysterically: 'Oh, look at my lovely boat, everyone! Look at my lovely boat! And the lights! Ha! ha! ha!' The voice went into hysterics of derisive laughter. We looked to see where the effusion came from, and saw a man in a rowing-boat, dressed in white flannels, with a lady reclining in the back seat. The ensemble was like a comic illustration from *Punch*. Karno leaned over the rail and gave him a very loud raspberry, but nothing deterred his hysterical laughter. 'There is only one thing to do,' I said: 'to be as vulgar as he thinks we are.' So I let out a violent flow of Rabelaisian invective, which was so embarrassing for his lady that he quickly rowed away.

The idiot's ridiculous outburst was not a criticism of taste, but a snobbish prejudice against what he considered lower-class ostentatiousness. He would never laugh hysterically at Buckingham Palace and scream: 'Oh, look what a big house I live in!' or laugh at the Coronation coach. This ever-present class tabulating I felt keenly while in England. It seems that this type of Englishman is only too quick to measure the other fellow's social inferiorities.

Our American troupe was put to work and for fourteen weeks we played the halls around London. The show was received well and the audiences were wonderful, but all the time I was wondering if we'd ever get back to the States again. I loved England, but it was impossible for me to live there; because of my background I had a disquieting feeling of sinking back into a depressing commonplaceness. So that when news came that we were booked for another tour in the States I was elated.

On Sunday Sydney and I saw Mother and she seemed in better health, and before Sydney left for the provinces we had supper together. On my last night in London, emotionally confused, sad, and embittered, I again walked about the West End, thinking to myself: 'This is the last time I shall ever see these streets.'

* * *

This time we arrived via New York on the *Olympic* second-class. The throb of the engines slowed down, signifying that we were approaching our destiny. This time I felt at home in the States—a foreigner among foreigners, allied with the rest.

As much as I liked New York I also looked forward to the West, to greeting again those acquaintances whom I now looked upon as warm friends: the Irish bar-tender in Butte, Montana, the cordial and hospitable real estate millionaire of Minneapolis, the beautiful girl in St Paul with whom I had spent a romantic week, MacAbee, the Scottish mine-owner of Salt Lake City, the friendly dentist in Tacoma, and in San Francisco, the Graumans.

Before going to the Pacific Coast we played around the 'smalls'—the small theatres around the outlying suburbs of Chicago and Philadelphia and industrial towns such as Fall River and Duluth, etc.

As usual I lived alone. But it had its advantages, because it gave me an opportunity to improve my mind, a resolution I had held for many months but never fulfilled.

There is a fraternity of those who passionately want to know. I was one of them. But my motives were not so pure;

I wanted to know, not for the love of knowledge but as a defence against the world's contempt for the ignorant. So when I had time I browsed around the second-hand bookshops.

In Philadelphia, I inadvertently came upon an edition of Robert Ingersoll's *Essays and Lectures*. That was an exciting discovery; his atheism confirmed my own belief that the horrific cruelty of the Old Testament was degrading to the human spirit. Then I discovered Emerson. After reading his essay on 'Self-Reliance' I felt I had been handed a golden birthright. Schopenhauer followed. I bought three volumes of *The World as Will and Idea*, which I have read on and off, never thoroughly, for over forty years. Walt Whitman's *Leaves of Grass* annoyed me and does to this day. He is too much the bursting heart of love, too much a national mystic. In my dressing-room between shows I also had the pleasure of meeting Twain, Poe, Hawthorne, Irving and Hazlitt. On that second tour I may not have absorbed as much classic education as I would have desired, but I did absorb a great deal of tedium in the lower strata of show business.

These cheap vaudeville circuits were bleak and depressing, and hopes about my future in America disappeared in the grind of doing three and sometimes four shows a day, seven days a week. Vaudeville in England was a paradise by comparison. At least we only worked there six days a week and only gave two shows a night. Our consolation was that in America we could save a little more money.

We had been working the 'sticks' continuously for five months and the weariness of it had left me discouraged, so that when we had a week's lay-off in Philadelphia, I welcomed it. I needed a change, another environment—to lose my identity and become someone else. I was fed up with the drab routine of tenth-rate vaudeville and decided that for one week I would indulge in the romance of graceful living. I had saved a considerable sum of money, and in sheer desperation, I decided to go on a spending spree. Why not? I had lived frugally to save it, and when out of work I would continue to live frugally on it; so why not spend a little of it now?

I bought an expensive dressing-gown and a smart over-night suitcase, which cost me seventy-five dollars. The shopkeeper was most courteous: 'Can we deliver them for you, sir?' Just his few words gave me a lift, a little distinction. Now I would go to New York and shed myself of tenth-rate vaudeville and its whole drab existence.

I took a room at the Hotel Astor which was quite grandiose in those days. I wore my smart cut-away coat and derby hat and cane, and of course carried my small suitcase. The splendour of the lobby and the confidence of the people strutting about it made me tremble slightly as I registered at the desk.

The room cost $4.50 a day. Timidly I asked if I should pay in advance. The clerk was most courteous and reassuring: 'Oh no, sir, it isn't necessary.'

Passing through the lobby with all its gilt and plush did something to me emotionally, so that when I reached my room I felt I wanted to weep. I stayed in it over an hour, inspecting the bathroom with its elaborate plumbing fixtures and testing its generous flush of hot and cold water. How bountiful and reassuring is luxury!

I took a bath and combed my hair and put on my new bathrobe, intending to get every ounce of luxury out of my four dollars fifty worth ... If only I had something to read, a newspaper. But I had not the confidence to telephone for one. So I took a chair and sat in the middle of the room surveying everything with a feeling of luxuriant melancholy.

After a while I dressed and went downstairs. I asked for the main dining-room. It was rather early for dinner; the place was almost empty but for one or two diners. The maître d'hôtel led me to a table by the window. 'Would you like to sit here, sir?'

'Anywhere will do,' I said in my best English voice.

Suddenly an industry of waiters whirled about me, delivering

143

ice water, the menu, the butter and bread. I was too emotional to be hungry. However, I went through the gestures and ordered consommé, roast chicken, and vanilla ice-cream for dessert. The waiter offered me a wine-list, and after careful scrutiny I ordered a half-bottle of champagne. I was too preoccupied living the part to enjoy the wine or the meal. After I had finished, I tipped the waiter a dollar, which was an extraordinarily generous tip in those days. But it was worth it for the bowing and attention I received on my way out. For no apparent reason I returned to my room and sat in it for ten minutes, then washed my hands and went out.

It was a soft summer evening in keeping with my mood as I walked sedately in the direction of the Metropolitan Opera House. *Tannhäuser* was playing there. I had never seen grand opera, only excerpts of it in vaudeville—and I loathed it. But now I was in the humour for it. I bought a ticket and sat in the second circle. The opera was in German and I did not understand a word of it, nor did I know the story. But when the dead Queen was carried on to the music of the Pilgrims' Chorus, I wept bitterly. It seemed to sum up all the travail of my life. I could hardly control myself; what people sitting next to me must have thought I don't know, but I came away limp and emotionally shattered.

I took a walk down town, choosing the darkest streets, as I could not cope with the vulgar glare of Broadway, nor could I return to that silly room at the hotel until my mood had worn off. When I recovered I intended going straight to bed. I was emotionally and physically exhausted.

As I entered the hotel I suddenly ran into Arthur Kelly, Hetty's brother, who used to be manager of the troupe that she was in. Because he was her brother I had cultivated him as a friend. I had not seen Arthur in several years.

'Charlie! Where are you going?' he said.

Nonchalantly I nodded in the direction of the Astor. 'I was about to go to bed.'

The effect was not lost on Arthur.

He was with two friends, and after introducing me he suggested that we should go to his apartment on Madison Avenue for a cup of coffee and a chat.

It was quite a comfortable flat and we sat around and made light conversation, Arthur carefully avoiding any reference to our past. Nevertheless, because I was staying at the Astor, he was curious to glean information. But I told him little, only that I had come to New York for two or three days' holiday.

Arthur had come a long way since living in Camberwell. He was now a prosperous business man working for his brother-in-law, Frank J. Gould. As I sat listening to his social chatter, it increased my melancholy. Said Kelly, referring to one of his friends: 'He's a nice chap, comes from a very good family, I understand.' I smiled to myself at his genealogical interest and realised that Arthur and I had little in common.

I stayed only one day in New York. The following morning I decided to return to Philadelphia. Although that one day had been the change I needed, it had been an emotional and a lonely one. Now I wanted company. I looked forward to our Monday morning performance and meeting members of the troupe. No matter how irksome it was returning to the old grind, that one day of graceful living had sufficed me.

When I got back to Philadelphia I dropped by the theatre. There was a telegram addressed to Mr Reeves, and I happened to be there when he opened it. 'I wonder if this means you,' he said. It read: 'Is there a man named Chaffin in your company or something like that stop if so will he communicate with Kessel and Bauman 24 Longacre Building Broadway.'

There was no one by that name in the company, but, as Reeves suggested, the name might mean Chaplin. Then I became excited, for Longacre Building, I discovered, was in the centre of Broadway and was full of lawyers' offices; remembering that I had a rich aunt somewhere in the States, my imagination took flight; she might have died and left me a fortune. So I wired back to Kessel and Bauman that there was a Chaplin in the company whom they perhaps meant. I waited anxiously for a reply. It came the same day. I tore open the telegram. It read: 'Will you have Chaplin call at our office as soon as possible?'

With excitement and anticipation, I caught the early morning train for New York, which was only two and a half hours from Philadelphia. I did not know what to expect—I imagined sitting in a lawyer's office listening to a will being read.

When I arrived, however, I was somewhat disappointed, for Kessel and Bauman were not lawyers but producers of motion pictures. However, the actual facts of the situation were to be thrilling.

Mr Charles Kessel, one of the owners of the Keystone Comedy Film Company, said that Mr Mack Sennett had seen me playing the drunk in the American Music Hall on Forty-second Street and if I were the same man he would like to engage me to take the place of Mr Ford Sterling. I had often played with the idea of working in films, and even offered to go into partnership with Reeves, our manager, to buy the rights of all Karno's sketches and make movies of them. But Reeves had been sceptical and sensibly so, because we knew nothing about making them.

Had I seen a Keystone Comedy? asked Mr Kessel. Of course, I had seen several, but I did not tell him that I thought they were a crude mélange of rough and tumble. However, a pretty, dark-eyed girl named Mabel Normand, who was quite charming, weaved in and out of them and justified their existence. I was not terribly enthusiastic about the Keystone type of comedy, but I realised their publicity value. A year at that racket and I could return to vaudeville an international star. Besides, it would mean a new life and a pleasant environment. Kessel said the contract would call for appearing in three films a week at a salary of one hundred and fifty dollars. This was twice what I was getting with the Karno Company. However,

I hemmed and hawed and said I could not accept less than two hundred dollars a week. Mr Kessel said that was up to Mr Sennett; he would notify him in California and let me know.

I did not exist while waiting to hear from Kessel. Perhaps I had asked too much? At last the letter came, stating they were willing to sign a year's contract for one hundred and fifty dollars the first three months and one hundred and seventy-five dollars for the remaining nine, more money than I had ever been offered in my life. It was to start with the termination of our Sullivan and Considine tour.

When we played the Empress in Los Angeles, we were a howling success, thank God. It was a comedy called *A Night at the Club*. I played a decrepit old drunk and looked at least fifty years old. Mr Sennett came round after the performance and congratulated me. In that short interview, I was aware of a heavy-set man with a beetling brow, a heavy, coarse mouth and a strong jaw, all of which impressed me. But I wondered how sympathetic he would be in our future relationship. All through that interview I was extremely nervous and was not sure whether he was pleased with me or not.

He asked casually when I would join them. I told him that I could start the first week in September, which would be the termination of my contract with the Karno Company.

I had qualms about leaving the troupe in Kansas City. The company was returning to England, and I to Los Angeles, where I would be on my own, and the feeling was not too reassuring. Before the last performance I ordered drinks for everyone and felt rather sad at the thought of parting.

A member of our troupe, Arthur Dando, who for some reason disliked me, thought he would play a joke and conveyed by whispered innuendoes that I was to receive a small gift from the company. I must confess I was touched by the thought. However, nothing happened. When everyone had left the dressing-room, Fred Karno Junior confessed that Dando had arranged to make a speech and present me with the gift, but after I had bought drinks for everyone he had not had the courage to go through with it and had left the so-called 'present' behind the dressing-table mirror. It was an empty tobacco-box, wrapped in tinfoil, containing small ends of old pieces of grease-paint.

X

EAGER and anxious, I arrived in Los Angeles and took a room at a small hotel, the Great Northern. The first evening I took a busman's holiday and saw the second show at the Empress, where the Karno Company had worked. The attendant recognised me and came a few moments later to tell me that Mr Sennett and Miss Mabel Normand were sitting two rows back and had asked if I would join them. I was thrilled, and after a hurried, whispered introduction we all watched the show together. When it was over, we walked a few paces down Main Street, and went to a rathskeller for a light supper and a drink. Mr Sennett was shocked to see how young I looked. 'I thought you were a much older man,' he said. I could detect a tinge of concern, which made me anxious, remembering that all Sennett's comedians were oldish-looking men. Fred Mace was over fifty and Ford Sterling in his forties. 'I can make up as old as you like,' I answered. Mabel Normand, however, was more reassuring. Whatever her reservations were about me, she did not reveal them. Mr Sennett said that I would not start immediately, but should come to the studio in Edendale and get acquainted with the people. When we left the café, we bundled into Mr Sennett's glamorous racing car and I was driven to my hotel.

The following morning I boarded a street-car for Edendale, a suburb of Los Angeles. It was an anomalous-looking place that could not make up its mind whether to be a humble residential district or a semi-industrial one. It had small lumber-yards and junk-yards, and abandoned-looking small farms on which were built one or two shacky wooden stores that fronted the road. After many enquiries I found myself opposite the Keystone Studio. It was a dilapidated affair with a green fence round it, one hundred and fifty feet square. The entrance to it was up a garden path through an old bungalow—

the whole place looked just as anomalous as Edendale itself. I stood gazing at it from the opposite side of the road, debating whether to go in or not.

It was lunch-time and I watched the men and women in their make-up come pouring out of the bungalow, including the Keystone Cops. They crossed the road to a small general store and came out eating sandwiches and hot dogs. Some called after each other in loud, raucous voices: 'Hey, Hank, come on!' 'Tell Slim to hurry!'

Suddenly I was seized with shyness and walked quickly to the corner at a safe distance, looking to see if Mr Sennett or Miss Normand would come out of the bungalow, but they did not appear. For half an hour I stood there, then decided to go back to the hotel. The problem of entering the studio and facing all those people became an insuperable one. For two days I arrived outside the studio, but I had not the courage to go in. The third day Mr Sennett telephoned and wanted to know why I had not shown up. I made some sort of excuse. 'Come down right away, we'll be waiting for you,' he said. So I went down and boldly marched into the bungalow and asked for Mr Sennett.

He was pleased to see me and took me immediately into the studio. I was enthralled. A soft even light pervaded the whole stage. It came from broad streams of white linen that diffused the sun and gave an ethereal quality to everything. This diffusion was for photographing in daylight.

After being introduced to one or two actors I became interested in what was going on. There were three sets side by side, and three comedy companies were at work in them. It was like viewing something at the World's Fair. In one set Mabel Normand was banging on a door shouting: 'Let me in!' Then the camera stopped and that was it—I had no idea films were made piecemeal in this fashion.

On another set was the great Ford Sterling whom I was to replace. Mr Sennett introduced me to him. Ford was leaving

Keystone to form his own company with Universal. He was immensely popular with the public and with everyone in the studio. They surrounded his set and were laughing eagerly at him.

Sennett took me aside and explained their method of working. 'We have no scenario—we get an idea then follow the natural sequence of events until it leads up to a chase, which is the essence of our comedy.'

This method was edifying, but personally I hated a chase. It dissipates one's personality; little as I knew about movies, I knew that nothing transcended personality.

That day I went from set to set watching the companies at work. They all seemed to be imitating Ford Sterling. This worried me, because his style did not suit me. He played a harassed Dutchman, ad-libbing through the scene with a Dutch accent, which was funny but was lost in silent pictures. I wondered what Sennett expected of me. He had seen my work and must have known that I was not suitable to play Ford's type of comedy; my style was just the opposite. Yet every story and situation conceived in the studio was consciously or unconsciously made for Sterling; even Roscoe Arbuckle was imitating Sterling.

The studio had evidently been a farm. Mabel Normand's dressing-room was situated in an old bungalow and adjoining it was another room where the ladies of the stock company dressed. Across from the bungalow was what had evidently been a barn, the main dressing-room for minor members of the stock company and the Keystone Cops, the majority of whom were ex-circus clowns and prize-fighters. I was allotted the star dressing-room used by Mack Sennett, Ford Sterling and Roscoe Arbuckle. It was another barn-like structure which might have been the harness-room. Besides Mabel Normand, there were several other beautiful girls. It was a strange and unique atmosphere of beauty and beast.

For days I wandered around the studio, wondering when I

would start work. Occasionally I would meet Sennett crossing the stage, but he would look through me, preoccupied. I had an uncomfortable feeling that he thought he had made a mistake in engaging me which did little to ameliorate my nervous tension.

Each day my peace of mind depended on Sennett. If perchance he saw me and smiled, my hopes would rise. The rest of the company had a wait-and-see attitude but some, I felt, considered me a doubtful substitute for Ford Sterling.

When Saturday came Sennett was most amiable. Said he: 'Go to the front office and get your cheque.' I told him I was more anxious to get to work. I wanted to talk about imitating Ford Sterling, but he dismissed me with the remark: 'Don't worry, we'll get round to that.'

Nine days of inactivity had passed and the tension was excruciating. Ford, however, would console me and after work he would occasionally give me a lift down-town, where we would stop in at the Alexandria Bar for a drink and meet several of his friends. One of them, a Mr Elmer Ellsworth, whom I disliked at first and thought rather crass, would jokingly taunt me: 'I understand you're taking Ford's place. Well, are you funny?'

'Modesty forbids,' I said squirmishly. This sort of ribbing was most embarrassing, especially in the presence of Ford. But he graciously took me off the hook with a remark. 'Didn't you catch him at the Empress playing the drunk? Very funny.'

'Well, he hasn't made me laugh yet,' said Ellsworth.

He was a big, cumbersome man, and looked glandular, with a melancholy, hangdog expression, hairless face, sad eyes, a loose mouth and a smile that showed two missing front teeth. Ford whispered impressively that he was a great authority on literature, finance and politics, one of the best-informed men in the country, and that he had a great sense of humour. However I did not appreciate it and would try to avoid him. But one night at the Alexandria bar, he said: 'Hasn't this limey got started yet?'

'Not yet,' I laughed uncomfortably.

'Well, you'd better be funny.'

Having taken a great deal from the gentleman, I gave him back some of his own medicine: 'Well, if I'm half as funny as you look, I'll do all right.'

'Blimey! A sarcastic wit, eh? I'll buy him a drink after that.'

       *   *   *

At last the moment came. Sennett was away on location with Mabel Normand as well as the Ford Sterling Company, so there was hardly anyone left in the studio. Mr Henry Lehrman, Keystone's top director after Sennett, was to start a new picture and wanted me to play a newspaper reporter. Lehrman was a vain man and very conscious of the fact that he had made some successful comedies of a mechanical nature; he used to say that he didn't need personalities, that he got all his laughs from mechanical effects and film-cutting.

We had no story. It was to be a documentary about the printing press done with a few comedy touches. I wore a light frock-coat, a top hat and a handlebar moustache. When we started I could see that Lehrman was groping for ideas. And of course being a newcomer at Keystone, I was anxious to make suggestions. This was where I created antagonism with Lehrman. In a scene in which I had an interview with an editor of a newspaper I crammed in every conceivable gag I could think of, even to suggesting business for others in the cast. Although the picture was completed in three days, I thought we contrived some very funny gags. But when I saw the finished film it broke my heart, for the cutter had butchered it beyond recognition, cutting into the middle of all my funny business. I was bewildered and wondered why they had done this. Henry Lehrman confessed years later that he had deliberately done it, because, as he put it, he thought I knew too much.

The day after I finished with Lehrman, Sennett returned from location. Ford Sterling was on one set, Arbuckle on another; the whole stage was crowded with three companies at work. I was in my street clothes and had nothing to do, so I stood where Sennett could see me. He was standing with Mabel, looking into a hotel lobby set, biting the end of a cigar. 'We need some gags here,' he said, then turned to me. 'Put on a comedy make-up. Anything will do.'

I had no idea what make-up to put on. I did not like my get-up as the press reporter. However, on the way to the wardrobe I thought I would dress in baggy pants, big shoes, a cane and a derby hat. I wanted everything a contradiction: the pants baggy, the coat tight, the hat small and the shoes large. I was undecided whether to look old or young, but remembering Sennett had expected me to be a much older man, I added a small moustache, which, I reasoned, would add age without hiding my expression.

I had no idea of the character. But the moment I was dressed, the clothes and the make-up made me feel the person he was. I began to know him, and by the time I walked on to the stage he was fully born. When I confronted Sennett I assumed the character and strutted about, swinging my cane and parading before him. Gags and comedy ideas went racing through my mind.

The secret of Mack Sennett's success was his enthusiasm. He was a great audience and laughed genuinely at what he thought funny. He stood and giggled until his body began to shake. This encouraged me and I began to explain the character: 'You know this fellow is many-sided, a tramp, a gentleman, a poet, a dreamer, a lonely fellow, always hopeful of romance and adventure. He would have you believe he is a scientist, a musician, a duke, a polo-player. However, he is not above picking up cigarette-butts or robbing a baby of its candy. And, of course, if the occasion warrants it, he will kick a lady in the rear—but only in extreme anger!'

I carried on this way for ten minutes or more, keeping Sennett in continuous chuckles. 'All right,' said he, 'get on the set and see what you can do there.' As with the Lehrman film, I knew little of what the story was about, other than that Mabel Normand gets involved with her husband and a lover.

In all comedy business an attitude is most important, but it is not always easy to find an attitude. However, in the hotel lobby I felt I was an impostor posing as one of the guests, but in reality I was a tramp just wanting a little shelter. I entered and stumbled over the foot of a lady. I turned and raised my hat apologetically, then turned and stumbled over a cuspidor, then turned and raised my hat to the cuspidor. Behind the camera they began to laugh.

Quite a crowd had gathered there, not only the players of the other companies who left their sets to watch us, but also the stage-hands, the carpenters and the wardrobe department. That indeed was a compliment. And by the time we had finished rehearsing we had quite a large audience laughing. Very soon I saw Ford Sterling peering over the shoulders of others. When it was over I knew I had made good.

At the end of the day when I went to the dressing-room, Ford Sterling and Roscoe Arbuckle were taking off their make-up. Very little was said, but the atmosphere was charged with cross-currents. Both Ford and Roscoe liked me, but I frankly felt they were undergoing some inner conflict.

It was a long scene that ran seventy-five feet. Later Mr Sennett and Mr Lehrman debated whether to let it run its full length, as the average comedy scene rarely ran over ten. 'If it's funny,' I said, 'does length really matter?' They decided to let the scene run its full seventy-five feet. As the clothes had imbued me with the character, I then and there decided I would keep to this costume whatever happened.

That evening I went home on the street-car with one of the small-bit players. Said he: 'Boy, you've started something; nobody ever got those kind of laughs on the set before, not even Ford Sterling—and you should have seen his face watching you, it was a study!'

'Let's hope they'll laugh the same way in the theatre,' I said, by way of suppressing my elation.

*   *   *

A few days later, at the Alexandria Bar, I overheard Ford giving his description of my character to our mutual friend Elmer Ellsworth: 'The guy has baggy pants, flat feet, the most miserable, bedraggled-looking little bastard you ever saw; makes itchy gestures as though he's got crabs under his arms—but he's funny.'

My character was different and unfamiliar to the American, and even unfamiliar to myself. But with the clothes on I felt he was a reality, a living person. In fact he ignited all sorts of crazy ideas that I would never have dreamt of until I was dressed and made up as the Tramp.

I became quite friendly with a small-bit player, and each night going home on the street-car he would give me a bulletin of the studio's reactions that day and talk of my comedy ideas. 'That was a wonderful gag, dipping your fingers in the finger-bowl, then wiping them on the old man's whiskers—they've never seen that kind of stuff around there.' And so he would carry on, having me stepping on air.

Under Sennett's direction I felt comfortable, because everything was spontaneously worked out on the set. As no one was positive or sure of himself (not even the director), I concluded that I knew as much as the other fellow. This gave me confidence; I began to offer suggestions which Sennett readily accepted. Thus grew a belief in myself that I was creative and could write my own stories. Sennett indeed had inspired this belief. But although I had pleased Sennett I had yet to please the public.

In the next picture I was assigned to Lehrman again. He was

156

leaving Sennett to join Sterling and to oblige Sennett was staying on two weeks longer than his contract called for. I still had abundant suggestions when I started working with him. He would listen and smile but would not accept any of them. 'That may be funny in the theatre,' he would say, 'but in pictures we have no time for it. We must be on the go—comedy is an excuse for a chase.'

I did not agree with this generality. 'Humour is humour,' I argued, 'whether in films or on the stage.' But he insisted on the same rigmarole, doing what the Keystone had always done. All action had to be fast—which meant running and climbing on top of the roofs of houses and street-cars, jumping into rivers and diving off piers. In spite of his comedy theories I happened to get in one or two bits of individual funny business, but, as before, he managed to have them mutilated in the cutting-room.

I do not think Lehrman gave a very promising report to Sennett about me. After Lehrman, I was assigned to another director, Mr Nichols, an oldish man in his late fifties who had been in motion pictures since their inception. I had the same trouble with him. He had but one gag, which was to take the comedian by the neck and bounce him from one scene to another. I tried to suggest subtler business, but he too would not listen. 'We have no time, no time!' he would cry. All he wanted was an imitation of Ford Sterling. Although I only mildly rebelled, it appears that he went to Sennett saying that I was a son of a bitch to work with.

About this time the picture which Sennett had directed, *Mabel's Strange Predicament*, was shown down-town. With fear and trepidation, I saw it with an audience. With Ford Sterling's appearance there was always a stir of enthusiasm and laughter, but I was received in cold silence. All the funny stuff I had done in the hotel lobby hardly got a smile. But as the picture progressed, the audience began to titter, then laugh, and towards the end of the picture there were one or two big laughs. At that showing I discovered that the audience were not partial to a newcomer.

I doubt whether this first effort came up to Sennett's expectations. I believe he was disappointed. He came to me a day or so later: 'Listen, they say you're difficult to work with.' I tried to explain that I was conscientious and was working only for the good of the picture. 'Well,' said Sennett, coldly, 'just do what you're told and we'll be satisfied.' But the following day I had another altercation with Nichols, and I blew up. 'Any three-dollar-a-day extra can do what you want me to do,' I declared. 'I want to do something with merit, not just be bounced around and fall off street-cars. I'm not getting a hundred and fifty dollars a week just for that.'

Poor old 'Pop' Nichols, as we called him, was in a terrible state. 'I've been in this business over ten years,' he said. 'What the hell do you know about it?' I tried to reason with him, but to no avail. I tried to reason with members of the cast, but they also were against me. 'Oh, he knows, he knows, he's been in the business much longer than you have,' said an old actor.

I made about five pictures and in some of them I had managed to put over one or two bits of comedy business of my own, in spite of the butchers in the cutting-room. Familiar with their method of cutting films, I would contrive business and gags just for entering and exiting from a scene, knowing that they would have difficulty in cutting them out. I took every opportunity I could to learn the business. I was in and out of the developing plant and cutting-room, watching the cutter piece the films together.

Now I was anxious to write and direct my own comedies, so I talked to Sennett about it. But he would not hear of it; instead he assigned me to Mabel Normand who had just started directing her own pictures. This nettled me, for, charming as Mabel was, I doubted her competence as a director; so the first day there came the inevitable blow-up. We were on location in the suburbs of Los Angeles and in one scene Mabel wanted me to stand with a hose and water down the road so that the villain's car would skid over it. I suggested standing on the hose so that the water can't come out, and when I look down the nozzle I unconsciously step off the hose and the water squirts in my face. But she shut me up quickly: 'We have no time! We have no time! Do what you're told.'

That was enough, I could not take it—and from such a pretty girl. 'I'm sorry, Miss Normand, I will not do what I'm told. I don't think you are competent to tell me what to do.'

The scene was in the centre of the road, and I left it and sat down on the kerb. Sweet Mabel—at that time she was only twenty, pretty and charming, everybody's favourite, everybody loved her. Now she sat by the camera bewildered; nobody had ever spoken to her so directly before. I also was susceptible to her charm and beauty and secretly had a soft spot in my heart for her, but this was my work. Immediately the staff and the cast surrounded Mabel and went into conference. One or two extras, Mabel told me afterwards, wanted to slug me, but she stopped them from doing so. Then she sent the assistant over to find out if I was going to continue working. I crossed the road to where she was sitting. 'I'm sorry,' I said apologetically, 'I just don't think it's funny or amusing. But if you'll allow me to offer a few comedy suggestions—.' She did not argue. 'Very well,' she said. 'If you won't do what you're told, we'll go back to the studio.' Although the situation was desperate I was resigned, so I shrugged. We had not lost much of the day's work, for we had been shooting since nine in the morning. It was now past five in the afternoon and the sun was sinking fast.

At the studio, while I was taking off my grease-paint, Sennett came bursting into the dressing-room. 'What the hell's the idea?' he said.

I tried to explain. 'The story needs gagging up,' I said, 'but Miss Normand will not listen to any suggestions.'

'You'll do what you're told or get out, contract or no contract,' he said.

I was very calm. 'Mr Sennett,' I answered, 'I earned my bread and cheese before I came here, and if I'm fired—well, I'm fired. But I'm conscientious and just as keen to make a good picture as you are.'

Without saying anything further he slammed the door.

That night going home on the street-car with my friend I told him what had happened.

'Too bad. You were going great there for a while,' he said.

'Do you think they'll fire me?' I said cheerfully, in order to hide my anxiety.

'I wouldn't be at all surprised. When I saw him leaving your dressing-room he looked pretty mad.'

'Well, it's O.K. with me. I've got fifteen hundred dollars in my belt and that will more than pay my fare back to England. However, I'll show up tomorrow and if they don't want me— *c'est la vie.*'

There was an eight o'clock call the following morning and I was not sure what to do, so I sat in the dressing-room without making up. About ten minutes to eight Sennett poked his head in the door. 'Charlie, I want to talk to you, let's go into Mabel's dressing-room.' His tone was surprisingly friendly.

'Yes, Mr Sennett,' I said, following him.

Mabel was not there; she was in the projection-room looking at rushes.

'Listen,' said Mack, 'Mabel's very fond of you, we all are fond of you and think you're a fine artist.'

I was surprised at this sudden change and I immediately began to melt. 'I certainly have the greatest respect and admiration for Miss Normand,' I said, 'but I don't think she is competent to direct—after all she's very young.'

'Whatever you think, just swallow your pride and help out,' said Sennett, patting me on the shoulder.

'That's precisely what I've been trying to do.'

160

28. Ballet Américain – the Keystone Cops

29. Prosperity came to the Keystone studios after I left

30. Roscoe Arbuckle

31. Mabel Normand

32. Ford Sterling

33. Mack Sennett

'Well, do your best to get along with her.'

'Listen, if you'll let me direct myself, you'll have no trouble,' I said.

Mack paused a moment. 'Who's going to pay for the film if we can't release it?'

'I will,' I answered. 'I'll deposit fifteen hundred dollars in any bank and if you can't release the picture you can keep the money.'

Mack thought a moment. 'Have you a story?'

'Of course, as many as you want.'

'All right,' said Mack, 'finish the picture with Mabel, then I'll see.' We shook hands in a most friendly manner. Later I went to Mabel and apologised, and that evening Sennett took us both out to dinner. The next day Mabel could not have been sweeter. She even came to me for suggestions and ideas. Thus, to the bewilderment of the camera crew and the rest of the cast, we happily completed the picture. Sennett's sudden change of attitude baffled me. It was months later, however, that I found out the reason: it appears that Sennett intended firing me at the end of the week, but the morning after I had quarrelled with Mabel, Mack received a telegram from the New York office telling him to hurry up with more Chaplin pictures as there was a terrific demand for them.

The average number of prints for a Keystone Comedy release was twenty. Thirty was considered quite successful. The last picture, which was the fourth one, reached forty-five copies, and demands for further copies were increasing. Hence Mack's friendliness after the telegram.

The mechanics of directing were simple in those days. I had only to know my left from my right for entrances and exits. If one exited right from a scene, one came in left in the next scene; if one exited towards the camera, one entered with one's back to the camera in the next scene. These, of course, were primary rules.

But with more experience I found that the placing of a

camera was not only psychological but articulated a scene; in fact it was the basis of cinematic style. If the camera is a little too near, or too far, it can enhance or spoil an effect. Because economy of movement is important you don't want an actor to walk any unnecessary distance unless there is a special reason, for walking is not dramatic. Therefore placement of camera should effect composition and a graceful entrance for the actor. Placement of camera is cinematic inflection. There is no set rule that a close-up gives more emphasis than a long shot. A close-up is a question of feeling; in some instances a long shot can effect greater emphasis.

An example of this is in one of my early comedies, *Skating*. The tramp enters the rink and skates with one foot up, gliding and twirling, tripping and bumping into people and getting into all sorts of mischief, eventually leaving everyone piled up on their backs in the foreground of the camera while he skates to the rear of the rink, becoming a very small figure in the background, and sits amongst the spectators innocently reviewing the havoc he has just created. Yet the small figure of the tramp in the distance was funnier than he would have been in a close-up.

When I started directing my first picture, I was not as confident as I thought I would be; in fact, I had a slight attack of panic. But after Sennett saw the first day's work I was reassured. The picture was called *Caught in the Rain*. It was not a world-beater, but it was funny and quite a success. When I finished it, I was anxious to know Sennett's reaction. I waited for him as he came out of the projection-room. 'Well, are you ready to start another?' he said. From then on I wrote and directed all my own comedies. As an inducement, Sennett gave me twenty-five dollars' bonus for each picture.

He now practically adopted me, and took me to dinner every night. He would discuss stories for the other companies with me and I would suggest crazy ideas which I felt were too personal to be understood by the public. But Sennett would laugh and accept them.

Now, when I saw my films with an audience, their reaction was different. The stir and excitement at the announcement of a Keystone Comedy, those joyful little screams that my first appearance evoked even before I had done anything, were most gratifying. I was a great favourite with the audience: if I could just continue this way of life I could be satisfied. With my bonus I was making two hundred dollars a week.

Since I was engrossed in work I had little time for the Alexandria Bar or my sarcastic friend, Elmer Ellsworth. I met him, however, weeks later, on the street. 'Say, listen,' said he, 'I've been seeing your pictures lately, and, by God, you're good! You have a quality entirely different from all the rest. And I'm not kidding. You're funny! Why the hell didn't you say so in the first place?' Of course, we became very good friends after that.

There was a lot Keystone taught me and a lot I taught Keystone. In those days they knew little about technique, stage-craft, or movement, which I brought to them from the theatre. They also knew little about natural pantomime. In blocking a scene, a director would have three or four actors blatantly stand in a straight line facing the camera, and, with the broadest gestures, one would pantomime 'I-want-to-marry-your-daughter' by pointing to himself, then to his ring finger, then to the girl. Their miming dealt little with subtlety or effectiveness, so I stood out in contrast. In those early movies, I knew I had many advantages, and that, like a geologist, I was entering a rich unexplored field. I suppose that was the most exciting period of my career, for I was on the threshold of something wonderful.

Success makes one endearing and I became the familiar friend of everyone in the studio. I was 'Charlie' to the extras, to the stage-hands, the wardrobe department, and the camera-men. Although I am not a fraterniser, this pleased me indeed, for I knew that this familiarity meant I was a success.

Now I had confidence in my ideas, and I can thank Sennett

for that, for although unlettered like myself, he had belief in his own taste, and such belief he instilled in me. His manner of working had given me confidence; it seemed right. His remark that first day at the studio: "We have no scenario. We get an idea, then follow the natural sequence of events" had stimulated my imagination.

*   *   *

Creating this way made films exciting. In the theatre I had been confined to a rigid, non-deviating routine of repeating the same thing night after night; once stage business had been tried out and set, one rarely attempted to invent new business. The only motivating thing about acting in the theatre was a good performance or a bad one. But films were freer. They gave me a sense of adventure. 'What do you think of this for an idea?' Sennett would say, or: 'There's a flood down town on Main Street.' Such remarks launched a Keystone comedy. It was this charming alfresco spirit that was a delight—a challenge to one's creativeness. It was so free and easy—no literature, no writers, we just had a notion around which we built gags, then made up the story as we went along.

For instance, in *His Prehistoric Past* I started with one gag, which was my first entrance. I appeared dressed as a pre-historic man wearing a bearskin, and, as I scanned the land-scape, I began pulling the hair from the bearskin to fill my pipe. This was enough of an idea to stimulate a prehistoric story, introducing love, rivalry, combat and chase. This was the method by which we all worked at Keystone.

I can trace the first prompting of desire to add another dimen-sion to my films besides that of comedy. I was playing in a picture called *The New Janitor*, in a scene in which the manager of the office fires me. In pleading with him to take pity on me and et me retain my job, I started to pantomime appealingly that I had a large family of little children. Although I was enacting mock sentiment, Dorothy Davenport, an old actress, was on the sidelines watching the scene, and during rehearsal I looked up

164

and to my surprise found her in tears. 'I know it's supposed to be funny,' she said, 'but you just make me weep.' She confirmed something I already felt: I had the ability to evoke tears as well as laughter.

The 'he-man' atmosphere of the studio would have been almost intolerable but for the pulchritudinous influence. Mabel Normand's presence, of course, graced the studio with glamour. She was extremely pretty, with large heavy-lidded eyes and full lips that curled delicately at the corners of her mouth, expressing humour and all sorts of indulgence. She was light-hearted and gay, a good fellow, kind and generous; and everyone adored her.

Stories went around of Mabel's generosity to the wardrobe woman's child, of the jokes she played on the camera-man. Mabel liked me in a sisterly fashion, for at that time she was very much enamoured of Mack Sennett. Because of Mack I saw a lot of Mabel; the three of us would dine together and afterwards Mack would fall asleep in the hotel lobby and we would while away an hour at the movies or in a café, then come back and wake him up. Such propinquity, one might think, would result in a romance, but it did not; we remained, unfortunately, only good friends.

Once, however, when Mabel, Roscoe Arbuckle and I appeared for some charity at one of the theatres in San Francisco, Mabel and I came very near to being emotionally involved. It was a glamorous evening and the three of us had appeared with great success at the theatre. Mabel had left her coat in the dressing-room and asked me to take her there to get it. Arbuckle and the others were waiting below outside in a car. For a moment we were alone. She looked radiantly beautiful and as I placed her wrap over her shoulders I kissed her and she kissed me back. We might have gone further, but people were waiting. Later I tried to follow up the episode, but nothing ever came of it. 'No, Charlie,' she said good-humouredly, 'I'm not your type, neither are you mine.'

About this time Diamond Jim Brady came to Los Angeles—
Hollywood was then in embryo. He arrived with the Dolly
Sisters and their husbands, and entertained lavishly. At a dinner
he gave at the Alexandria Hotel there were the Dolly Twins and
their husbands, Carlotta Monterey, Lou Tellegen, leading man
of Sarah Bernhardt, Mack Sennett, Mabel Normand, Blanche
Sweet, Nat Goodwin and many others. The Dolly Twins were
sensationally beautiful. The two of them, their husbands and
Diamond Jim Brady were almost inseparable; their association
was puzzling.

Diamond Jim was a unique American character, who looked
like a benign John Bull. That first night I could not believe
my eyes, for he wore diamond cuff-links and studs in his
shirtfront, each stone larger than a shilling. A few nights
later we dined at Nat Goodwin's Café on the pier, and this
time Diamond Jim showed up with his emerald set, each
stone the size of a small matchbox. At first I thought he was
wearing them as a joke, and innocently asked if they were
genuine. He said they were. 'But,' I said, with astonishment,
'they are fabulous.' 'If you want to see beautiful emeralds, here,'
he replied. He lifted his dress waistcoat, showing a belt the size
of the Marquess of Queensberry's championship belt, completely
covered with the largest emeralds I have ever seen. He was
quite proud to tell me that he had ten sets of precious stones
and wore a different set every night.

It was 1914 and I was twenty-five years old, in the flush of
youth and enamoured with my work, not alone for the
success of it, but for its enchantment, as it gave me an opportunity of meeting all the film stars—and I was their fan at one
time or other. Mary Pickford, Blanche Sweet, Miriam Cooper,
Clara Kimball Young, the Gish sisters and others—all of them
beautiful, and actually to meet them face to face was Elysian.

Thomas Ince gave barbecues and dances at his studio, which
was in the wilds of northern Santa Monica, facing the Pacific
Ocean. What wondrous nights—youth and beauty dancing to

plaintive music on an open-air stage, with the soft sound of waves pounding on the nearby shore.

Peggy Pierce, an exceptionally beautiful girl with delicately chiselled features, beautiful white neck and a ravishing figure, was my first heart-throb. She did not make her appearance until my third week at the Keystone, having been ill with 'flu. But the moment we met we ignited; it was mutual, and my heart sang. How romantic were those mornings, turning up for work with the anticipation of seeing her each day.

On Sunday I would call for her at her parents' apartment. Each night we met was an avowal of love, each night was a struggle. Yes, Peggy loved me, but it was a lost cause. She resisted and resisted, until I gave up in despair. At that time I had no desire to marry anyone. Freedom was too much of an adventure. No woman could measure up to that vague image I had in my mind.

Each studio was like a family. Films were made in a week, feature-length films never took more than two or three weeks. We worked by sunlight, which was why we worked in California: it was known to have nine months of sunshine each year.

Klieg lights came in about 1915; but Keystone never used them because they wavered, were not as clear as sunlight, and the lamps took up too much time to arrange. A Keystone Comedy rarely took more than a week to make, in fact I had made one in an afternoon, a picture called *Twenty Minutes of Love*, and it was a continuous laugh throughout. *Dough and Dynamite*, a most successful film, took nine days, at a cost of eighteen hundred dollars. And because I went over the budget of one thousand dollars, which was the limit for a Keystone comedy, I lost my bonus of twenty-five dollars. The only way they could retrieve themselves, said Sennett, would be to put it out as a two-reeler, which they did, and it grossed more than one hundred and thirty thousand dollars the first year.

*   *   *

167

Now I had several successful pictures under my belt, including *Twenty Minutes of Love, Dough and Dynamite, Laughing Gas,* and *The Stage Hand.* During this time Mabel and I starred in a feature picture with Marie Dressler. It was pleasant working with Marie, but I did not think the picture had much merit. I was more than happy to get back to directing myself again.

I recommended Sydney to Sennett; as the name Chaplin was being featured, he was only too pleased to annex another member of our family. Sennett signed him up for a year at a salary of two hundred dollars a week, which was twenty-five dollars more than I was getting. Sydney and his wife, fresh from England, came to the studio as I was leaving for location. Later that evening we dined together. I enquired how my pictures went in England.

Before my name was advertised, he said, many music-hall artists had spoken enthusiastically to him about a new American cinema comedian they had just seen. He also told me that before he had seen any of my comedies he called up the film exchange to find out when they would be released and, when he told them who he was, they invited him to see three of them. He had sat alone in the projection room and laughed like the devil.

'What was your reaction to all this?' I asked him.

Sydney expressed no great wonderment. 'Oh, I knew you'd make good,' he said confidently.

Mack Sennett was a member of the Los Angeles Athletic Club, which entitled him to give a temporary membership card to a friend, and he gave one to me. It was the headquarters of all the bachelors and business men in town, an elaborate club with a large dining-room and lounge rooms on the first floor, which were open to the ladies in the evening, and a cocktail bar.

I had a large corner room on the top floor, with a piano and a small library, next to Mose Hamberger, who owned the May Department Store (the largest in town). The cost of living was remarkably cheap in those days. I paid twelve dollars a week for my room, which gave me the use of all the facilities of the club, including elaborate gymnasiums, swimming pools and excellent service. All told, I lived in a sumptuous style for seventy-five dollars a week, out of which I kept my end up in rounds of drinks and occasional dinners.

There was a camaraderie about the club which even the declaration of the First World War did not disturb. Everyone thought it would be over in six months; that it would last for four years, as Lord Kitchener predicted, people thought preposterous. Many were rather glad that war had been declared, for now we would show the Germans. There was no question of the outcome; the English and the French would lick them in six months. The war had not really got into its stride and California was far away from the scene of action.

About this time Sennett began to talk of renewing my contract, and wanted to know my terms. I knew to some degree the extent of my popularity, but I also knew the ephemera of it, and believed that, at the rate I was going, within a year I would be all dried up, so I had to make hay while the sun shone. 'I want one thousand dollars per week!' I said deliberately.

Sennett was appalled. 'But *I* don't make that,' he said.

'I know it,' I answered, 'but the public doesn't line up outside the box-office when your name appears as they do for mine.'

'Maybe,' said Sennett, 'but without the support of our organisation you'd be lost.' He warned: 'Look what's happening to Ford Sterling.'

This was true, for Ford had not fared very well since leaving Keystone. But I told Sennett: 'All I need to make a comedy is a park, a policeman and a pretty girl.' As a matter of fact I had made some of my most successful pictures with just about that assembly.

Sennett, in the meantime, had wired to Kessel and Bauman, his partners, for advice about my contract and my demand. Later Sennett came to me with a proposition: 'Listen, you have four months to go. We'll tear up your contract and give you five hundred dollars now, seven hundred for the next year, and fifteen hundred for the following year. That way you'll get your thousand dollars a week.'

'Mack,' I answered, 'if you'll just reverse the terms, give me fifteen hundred the first year, seven hundred the second year, and five hundred the third, I'll take it.'

'But that's a crazy idea,' said Sennett.

So the question of a new contract was not discussed again.

*　　　*　　　*

I had a month to go with Keystone, and so far no other company had made me an offer. I was getting nervous and I fancy Sennett knew it and was biding his time. Usually he came to me at the end of a picture and jokingly hustled me up about starting another; now, although I had not worked for two weeks, he kept away from me. He was polite, but aloof.

In spite of the fact, my confidence never left me. If nobody made me an offer I would go into business for myself. Why not? I was confident and self-reliant. I remember the exact moment that feeling was born: I was signing a requisition slip against the studio wall.

After Sydney joined the Keystone Company, he made several successful films. One that broke records throughout the world was *The Submarine Pirate*, in which Sydney contrived all sorts of camera tricks. As he was so successful, I approached him about joining me and starting our own company. 'All we need is a camera and a back lot,' I said. But Sydney was conservative. He thought it was taking too much of a chance. 'Besides,' he added, 'I don't feel like giving up a salary which is more than I have ever earned in my life.' So he continued with Keystone for another year.

One day I received a telephone call from Carl Laemmle of the Universal Company. He was willing to give me twelve cents a foot and finance my pictures, but he would not give me a salary of a thousand dollars a week, so nothing came of it.

A young man named Jess Robbins, who represented the Essanay Company, said he had heard that I wanted a ten-thousand-dollar bonus before signing a contract, and twelve hundred and fifty dollars a week. This was news to me. I had never thought of a ten-thousand-dollar bonus until he mentioned it, but from that happy moment it became a fixation in my mind.

That night I invited Robbins to dinner and let him do all the talking. He said that he had come directly from Mr G. M. Anderson, known as Bronco Billy, of the Essanay Company, who was a partner of Mr George K. Spoor, with an offer of twelve hundred and fifty dollars a week, but he was not sure about the bonus. I shrugged. 'That seems to be a hitch with so many of them,' I said. 'They're all full of big offers, but they don't put up any cash.' Later, he telephoned to Anderson in San Francisco, telling him that the deal was on, but that I wanted ten thousand dollars down as a bonus. He returned to the table all glowing. 'The deal's on,' he said, 'and you get your ten thousand dollars tomorrow.'

I was elated. It seemed too good to be true. Alas, it was, for the next day Robbins handed me a cheque for only six hundred dollars, explaining that Mr Anderson was coming himself to Los Angeles and that the matter of the ten thousand dollars would be taken care of then. Anderson arrived full of enthusiasm and assurance about the deal, but no ten thousand dollars. 'My partner, Mr Spoor, will attend to that when we get to Chicago.'

Although my suspicions were aroused, I preferred to bury them in optimism. I had two more weeks to go with Keystone. Finishing my last picture, *His Prehistoric Past*, was a strain, because it was hard to concentrate with so many business propositions dangling before me. Nevertheless, the picture was eventually completed.

IT was a wrench leaving Keystone, for I had grown fond of Sennett and everyone there. I never said goodbye to anyone, I couldn't. It all happened in a ruthlessly simple way. I finished cutting my film on Saturday night and left with Mr Anderson the following Monday for San Francisco, where we were met by his new green Mercedes car. We paused only for lunch at the St Francis Hotel, then went on to Niles, where Anderson had his own small studio in which he made his Bronco Billy Westerns for the Essanay Company (Essanay, a corruption, standing for the initials of Spoor and Anderson).

Niles was an hour's drive outside San Francisco, situated along the railroad track. It was a small town with a population of four hundred and its preoccupation was alfalfa and cattle-raising. The studio was situated in the centre of a field, about four miles outside. When I saw it my heart sank, for nothing could have been less inspiring. It had a glassed-in roof, which made it extremely hot when working in the summer. Anderson said that I would find the studios in Chicago more to my liking and better equipped for making comedies. I stayed only an hour in Niles while Anderson transacted some business with his staff. Then we both left for San Francisco again, where we embarked for Chicago.

I liked Anderson; he had a special kind of charm. On the train he tended me like a brother, and at the different stops would buy magazines and candy. He was shy and uncommunicative, a man about forty, and when business was discussed would magnanimously remark: 'Don't worry about that. It'll be O.K.' He had little conversation and was very much preoccupied. Yet I felt underneath he was shrewd.

The journey was interesting. On the train were three men. We first noticed them in the dining-car. Two looked quite prosperous, but the third looked out of place, a common, rough-looking fellow. It was strange to see them dining together. We speculated that the two might be engineers and the derelict-looking one a labourer to do the rough work. When we left the dining-car, one of them came to our compartment and introduced himself. He said he was sheriff of St Louis and had recognised Bronco Billy. They were transferring a criminal from San Quentin prison back to St Louis to be hanged, but, since they could not leave the prisoner alone, would we mind coming to their compartment to meet the district attorney?

'Thought you might like to know the circumstances,' said the sheriff confidentially. 'This fellow had quite a criminal record. When the officer arrested him in St Louis, he asked to be allowed to go to his room and take some clothes from his trunk; and while he was going through his trunk he suddenly whipped round with a gun and shot the officer dead, then escaped to California, where he was caught burglaring and was sentenced to three years. When he came out the district attorney and I were waiting for him. It's a cut-and-dried case—we'll hang him,' he said complacently.

Anderson and I went to their compartment. The sheriff was a jovial, thickset man, with a perpetual smile and a twinkle in his eye. The district attorney was more serious.

'Sit down,' said the sheriff, after introducing us to his friend. Then he turned to the prisoner. 'And this is Hank,' he said. 'We're taking him back to St Louis, where he's in a bit of a jam.'

Hank laughed ironically, but made no comment. He was a man six feet tall, in his late forties. He shook hands with Anderson, saying: 'I seen you many times, Bronco Billy, and, by God, the way you handle them guns and them stick-ups is the best I've ever seen.' Hank knew little about me, he said; he had been in San Quentin for three years—'and a lot goes on on the outside that you don't get to know about.'

Although we were all convivial there was an underlying tension which was difficult to cope with. I was at a loss what to say, so I just grinned at the sheriff's remarks.

'It's a tough world,' said Bronco Billy.

'Well,' said the sheriff, 'we want to make it less tough. Hank knows that.'

'Sure,' said Hank, brusquely.

The sheriff began moralising: 'That's what I told Hank when he stepped out of San Quentin. I said if he'll play square with us, we'll play square with him. We don't want to use handcuffs or make a fuss; all he's got on is a leg-iron.'

'A leg-iron! What's that?' I asked.

'Haven't you ever seen one?' said the sheriff. 'Lift up your trouser, Hank.'

Hank lifted his trouser-leg and there it was, a nickel-plated cuff about five inches in length and three inches thick, fitting snugly around his ankle, weighing forty pounds. This led to commenting on the latest type of leg-irons. The sheriff explained that this particular one had rubber insulation on the inside so as to make it easier for the prisoner.

'Does he sleep with that thing?' I asked.

'Well, that depends,' said the sheriff, looking coyly at Hank. Hank's smile was grim and cryptic.

We sat with them till dinner-time and as the day wore on the conversation turned to the manner in which Hank had been re-arrested. From the interchange of prison information, the sheriff explained, they had received photographs and finger-prints and decided that Hank was their man. So they had arrived outside the prison gates of San Quentin the day Hank was to be released.

'Yes,' said the sheriff, his small eyes twinkling and looking at Hank, 'we waited for him on the opposite side of the road. Very soon Hank came out of the side door of the prison gate.' The sheriff slid his index finger along the side of his nose and slyly pointed in the direction of Hank and with a diabolical grin said slowly: 'I—think—that's—our man!'

Anderson and I sat fascinated as he continued. 'So we made a deal,' said the sheriff, 'that if he'd play square with us, we'd

174

treat him right. We took him to breakfast and gave him hot cakes and bacon and eggs. And here he is, travelling first class. That's better than going the hard way in handcuffs and chains.'

Hank smiled and mumbled: 'I could have fought you on extradition if I'd wanted to.'

The sheriff eyed him coldly. 'That wouldn't have done you much good, Hank,' he said slowly. 'It would just have meant a little delay. Isn't it better to go first class in comfort?'

'I guess so,' said Hank, jerkily.

As we neared Hank's destination, he began to talk about the jail in St Louis almost with affection. He rather enjoyed the anticipation of his trial by the other prisoners: 'I'm just thinking what those gorillas will do to me when I get before the Kangaroo Court! Guess they'll take all my tobacco and cigarettes away from me.'

The sheriff's and the attorney's relationship with Hank was like a matador's fondness for the bull he is about to kill. When they left the train, it was the last day of December, and as we parted the sheriff and the attorney wished us a happy New Year. Hank also shook hands, saying grimly that all good things must come to an end. It was difficult to know how to bid him goodbye. His crime had been a ruthless and cowardly one, yet I found myself wishing him good luck as he limped from the train with his heavy leg-iron. Eventually we heard that he was hanged.

*   *   *

When we arrived in Chicago, we were greeted by the studio manager, but no Mr Spoor. Mr Spoor, he said, was away on business and would not return until after the New Year holiday. I did not think Spoor's absence had any significance then, because nothing would happen at the studio until after the first of the year. Meanwhile I spent New Year's Eve with Anderson, his wife and family. On New Year's Day Anderson left for California, assuring me that as soon as Spoor returned he would attend to everything, including the ten-thousand-dollar bonus. The studio was in the industrial district, and, at one time, had evidently been a warehouse. The morning I showed up there, no Spoor had yet arrived, nor were there any instructions left about my business arrangements. Immediately I sensed that something was fishy and that the office knew more than they cared to divulge. But it didn't worry me; I was confident that a good picture would solve all my problems. So I asked the manager if he knew that I was to get the full co-operation of the studio staff and *carte blanche* for all their facilities. 'Of course,' he replied. 'Mr Anderson has left instructions about that.'

'Then I would like to start work immediately,' I said.

'Very well,' he answered. 'On the first floor you will find the head of the scenario department, Miss Louella Parsons, who will give you a script.'

'I don't use other people's scripts, I write my own,' I snapped.

I was belligerent because they seemed so vague about everything and because of Spoor's absence; besides, the studio personnel were stuffy and went around like bank clerks, carrying requisition papers as though they were members of the Guaranty Trust Company—the business end of it was very impressive, but not their films. In the upstairs office the different departments were partitioned like tellers' grilles. It was anything but conducive to creative work. At six o'clock, no matter whether a director was in the middle of a scene or not, the lights were turned off and everybody went home.

The next morning I went to the casting grille. 'I would like a cast of some sort,' I said dryly, 'so will you kindly send me members of your company who are unoccupied?'

They presented people whom they thought might be suitable. There was a chap with cross eyes named Ben Turpin, who seemed to know the ropes and was not doing much with Essanay at the time. Immediately I took a liking to him, so he was chosen. But I had no leading lady. After I had had several

34. The Tramp makes his first appearance,
with Mabel Normand in *Mabel's Strange Predicament*

35. With Roscoe Arbuckle in *The Rounders*

36. *Burlesque on Carmen*

37. Edna Purviance

38. G. M. Anderson, known as
Bronco Billy, of the Essanay Company,
who gave me my first bonus of $600

39. President Freuler of the Mutual
Film Company handing me a $150,000
bonus a year later

interviews, one applicant seemed a possibility, a rather pretty young girl whom the company had just signed up. But oh, God! I could not get a reaction out of her. She was so unsatisfactory that I gave up and dismissed her. Gloria Swanson years later told me that she was the girl and that, having dramatic aspirations and hating slapstick comedy, she had been deliberately unco-operative.

Francis X. Bushman, then a great star with Essanay, sensed my dislike of the place. 'Whatever you think about the studio,' he said, 'it is just the antithesis': but it wasn't; I didn't like the studio and I didn't like the word 'antithesis'. Circumstances went from bad to worse. When I wanted to see my rushes, they ran the original negative to save the expense of a positive print. This horrified me. And when I demanded that they should make a positive print, they reacted as though I wanted to bankrupt them. They were smug and self-satisfied. Having been one of the first to enter the film business, and being protected by patent rights which gave them a monopoly, their last consideration was the making of good pictures. And although other companies were challenging their patent rights and making better films, Essanay still went smugly on, dealing out scenarios like playing cards every Monday morning.

I had almost finished my first picture, which was called *His New Job*, and two weeks had elapsed and still no Mr Spoor had shown up. Having received neither the bonus nor my salary, I was contemptuous. 'Where is this Mr Spoor?' I demanded at the front office. They were embarrassed and could give no satisfactory explanation. I made no effort to hide my contempt and asked if he always conducted his business affairs in this way.

Years later I heard from Spoor himself what had happened. It appears that when Spoor, who had never heard of me at that time, learned that Anderson had signed me up for a year at twelve hundred dollars a week with a ten-thousand-dollar bonus, he sent Anderson a frantic wire, wanting to know if he had gone mad. And when Spoor heard that Anderson had signed me purely as a gamble, on the recommendation of Jess Robbins, his anxiety was twofold. He had comics who were getting only seventy-five dollars a week, the best of them, and their comedies barely paid for themselves. Hence Spoor's absence from Chicago.

When he returned, however, he lunched at one of the big Chicago hotels with several friends who, to his surprise, complimented him about my joining his company. Also, more than the usual publicity began piling up in the studio office about Charlie Chaplin. So he thought he would try an experiment. He gave a page-boy a quarter and had me paged throughout the hotel. As the boy went through the lobby shouting: 'Call for Mr Charlie Chaplin,' people began to congregate until it was packed with stir and excitement. This was his first indication of my popularity. The second was what had happened at the film exchange while he was away: he discovered that even before I had started the picture there was an advance sale of sixty-five copies, something unprecedented, and by the time I had finished the film a hundred and thirty prints were sold and orders were still pouring in. Immediately they raised the price from thirteen cents to twenty-five cents a foot.

When Spoor eventually showed up, I confronted him about my salary and bonus. He was profuse with apologies, explaining that he had told the front office to take care of all business arrangements. He had not seen the contract, but assumed that the front office knew all about it. This cock-and-bull story infuriated me. 'What were you scared about?' I said, laconically. 'You can still get out of your contract if you wish—in fact I think you've already broken it.'

Spoor was a tall, portly individual, soft-spoken and almost good-looking but for a pale flabbiness of face and an acquisitive top lip that sat over the lower one.

'I'm sorry you feel this way,' he said, 'but, as you must know, Charlie, we are a reputable firm and always live up to our contract.'

'Well, you haven't lived up to this one,' I interposed.

'We'll take care of that matter right now,' he said.

'I'm in no hurry,' I answered, sarcastically.

*   *   *

During my short stay in Chicago, Spoor did everything to placate me, but I could never really warm up to him. I told him I was unhappy working in Chicago and that if he wanted results he should arrange for me to work in California. 'We'll do everything we can to make you happy,' he said. 'How would you like to go to Niles?'

I was not too pleased at the prospect, but I liked Anderson better than Spoor; so after the completing of *His New Job* I went to Niles.

Bronco Billy made all his Western movies there; they were one-reelers that took him a day to make. He had seven plots which he repeated over and over again, and from which he made several million dollars. He would work sporadically. Sometimes he would turn out seven one-reel Westerns in a week, then go on holiday for six weeks.

Surrounding the studio at Niles were several small Californian bungalows which Bronco Billy had built for members of his company, and a large one which he occupied himself. He told me that if I desired I could live there with him. I was delighted at the prospect. Living with Bronco Billy, the millionaire cowboy who had entertained me in Chicago at his wife's sumptuous apartment, would at least make life tolerable in Niles.

It was dark when we entered his bungalow, and when we switched on the light I was shocked. The place was empty and drab. In his room was an old iron bed with a light-bulb hanging over the head of it. A rickety old table and one chair were the other furnishings. Near the bed was a wooden box upon which was a brass ash-tray filled with cigarette-butts. The room allotted to me was almost the same, only it was minus a grocery box. Nothing worked. The bathroom was unspeakable. One had to take a jug and fill it from the bath tap and empty it down the flush to make the toilet work. This was the home of G. M. Anderson, the multi-millionaire cowboy.

I came to the conclusion that Anderson was an eccentric. Although a millionaire, he cared little for graceful living; his indulgences were flamboyant-coloured cars, promoting prize-fighters, owning a theatre and producing musical shows. When he was not working in Niles, he spent most of his time in San Francisco, where he stayed in small moderate-priced hotels. He was an odd fellow, vague, erratic and restless, who sought a solitary life of pleasure; and although he had a charming wife and daughter in Chicago, he rarely saw them. They lived their lives separately and apart.

It was disturbing moving again from one studio to another. I had to organise another working unit, which meant selecting a satisfactory camera-man, an assistant director and a stock company, the latter being difficult because there was little to choose from in Niles. There was one other company at Niles besides Anderson's cowboy outfit: this was a nondescript comedy company that kept things going and paid expenses when G. M. Anderson was not working. The stock company consisted of twelve people, and these were mostly cowboy actors. Again I had the problem of finding a pretty girl for a leading lady. Now I was anxious to get to work. Although I hadn't a story, I ordered the crew to build an ornate café set. When I was lost for a gag or an idea a café would always supply one. While it was being built I went with G. M. Anderson to San Francisco to look for a leading lady among the chorus girls of his musical comedy, and, although it was nice work, none of them was photogenic. Carl Strauss, a handsome young German-American cowboy working with Anderson, said he knew of a girl who occasionally went to Tate's Café on Hill Street. He did not know her personally, but she was pretty and the proprietor might know her address.

Mr Tate knew her quite well. She lived with her married

sister, she was from Lovelock, Nevada, her name was Edna Purviance. Immediately we got in touch with her and made an appointment to meet her at the St Francis Hotel. She was more than pretty, she was beautiful. At the interview she seemed sad and serious. I learned afterwards that she was just getting over a love affair. She had been to college and had taken a business course. She was quiet and reserved, with beautiful large eyes, beautiful teeth and a sensitive mouth. I doubted whether she could act or had any humour, she looked so serious. Nevertheless, with these reservations we engaged her. She would at least be decorative to my comedies.

The next day we returned to Niles, but the café was not ready, and what they had built was crude and awful; the studio was certainly lacking technically. After giving orders for a few alterations, I began to think of an idea. I thought of a title: *His Night Out*—a drunk in pursuit of pleasure—that was enough to start with. I added a fountain to the night-club, feeling I could get some gags out of it, and I had Ben Turpin as a stooge. The day before we started the picture a member of Anderson's company invited me to a supper party. It was a modest affair, with beer and sandwiches. There were about twenty of us, including Miss Purviance. After supper some played cards while others sat around and talked. We got on to the subject of hypnotism and I bragged about my hypnotic powers. I boasted that within sixty seconds I could hypnotise anyone in the room. I was so convincing that most of the company believed me, but Edna did not.

She laughed. 'What nonsense! No one could hypnotise me!'

'You,' I said, 'are just the perfect subject. I bet you ten dollars that I'll put you to sleep in sixty seconds.'

'All right,' said Edna, 'I'll bet.'

'Now, if you're not well afterwards don't blame me for it—of course it will be nothing serious.'

I tried to scare her into backing out, but she was resolute. One woman begged her not to allow it. 'You're very foolish,' she told her.

'The bet still goes,' said Edna, quietly.

'Very well,' I answered. 'I want you to stand with your back firmly against the wall, away from everybody, so that I can get your undivided attention.'

She obeyed, smiling superciliously. By this time everyone in the room was interested.

'Somebody watch the time,' I said.

'Remember,' said Edna, 'you're to put me to sleep in sixty seconds.'

'In sixty seconds you will be completely unconscious,' I answered.

'Go!' said the time-keeper.

Immediately I made two or three dramatic passes, staring intensely into her eyes. Then I came near to her face and whispered so that the others could not hear: 'Fake it!' and made passes, saying: 'You will be unconscious—you are unconscious, unconscious!'

Then I drew back and she began to stagger. Quickly I caught her in my arms. Two of the onlookers screamed. 'Quick!' I said. 'Someone help me put her on the couch.'

When she came to, she feigned bewilderment and said she felt tired. Although she could have won her argument and proved her point to all present, she had generously relinquished her triumph for the sake of a good joke. This won her my esteem and affection and convinced me that she had a sense of humour.

I made four comedies at Niles, but as the studio facilities were not satisfactory, I did not feel settled or contented there, so I suggested to Anderson my going to Los Angeles, where they had better facilities for making comedies. He agreed, but also for another reason: because I was monopolising the studio, which was not big enough or adequately staffed for three companies. So he negotiated the renting of a small studio at Boyle Heights, which was in the heart of Los Angeles.

While we were there, two young men who were just beginning in the business came and rented studio space, named Hal Roach and Harold Lloyd.

As the value of my comedies increased with every new picture, Essanay began demanding unprecedented terms, charging exhibitors a minimum of fifty dollars a day rental for my two-reel comedies. This meant that they were collecting over fifty thousand dollars in advance for each picture.

One evening, after I had returned to the Stoll Hotel, where I was staying, a middle-rate place but new and comfortable, there was an urgent telephone call from the Los Angeles *Examiner*. They read a telegram they had received from New York stating:

> Will give Chaplin $25,000 for two weeks
> to appear fifteen minutes each evening at
> the New York Hippodrome. This will not
> interfere with his work.

Immediately I put in a call to G. M. Anderson in San Francisco. It was late and I was not able to reach him until three in the morning. Over the phone I told him of the telegram and asked if he would let me off for two weeks in order to earn that twenty-five thousand dollars. I suggested that I could start a comedy on the train going to New York, and while there finish it. But Anderson did not want me to do it.

My bedroom window opened out on the well of the hotel, so that the voice of anyone talking resounded through the rooms. The telephone connection was bad,—'I don't intend to pass up twenty-five thousand dollars for two weeks' work!' I had to shout several times.

A window opened above and a voice shouted back: 'Cut out that bull and go to sleep, you big dope!'

Anderson said over the phone that, if I gave Essanay another two-reeler comedy, they would give me the twenty-five thousand. He agreed to come to Los Angeles the following day and give me the cheque and draw up an agreement. After I had finished telephoning I turned off the light and was about to go to sleep, then, remembering the voice, I got out of bed, opened the window and shouted up: 'Go to hell!'

Anderson came to Los Angeles the following day with a cheque for twenty-five thousand dollars, and the New York company that made the original offer went bankrupt two weeks later. Such was my luck.

Now back in Los Angeles I was much happier. Although the studio at Boyle Heights was in a slummy neighbourhood, it enabled me to be near my brother, whom I occasionally saw in the evening. He was still at Keystone and would finish his contract there about a month earlier than the completion of mine with Essanay. My success had taken on such proportions that Sydney now intended devoting his whole time to my business affairs. According to reports, my popularity kept increasing with each succeeding comedy. Although I knew the extent of my success in Los Angeles by the long lines at the box-office, I did not realise to what magnitude it had grown elsewhere. In New York, toys and statuettes of my character were being sold in all the department stores and drugstores. Ziegfeld Follies Girls were doing Chaplin numbers, marring their beauty with moustaches, derby hats, big shoes and baggy trousers, singing a song called *Those Charlie Chaplin Feet*.

We were also inundated with all manner of business propositions involving books, clothes, candles, toys, cigarettes and toothpaste. Also stacks upon stacks of increasing fanmail became a problem. Sydney insisted that it should all be answered, in spite of the expense of having to engage an extra secretary.

Sydney spoke to Anderson about selling my pictures separately from the rest of the routine product. It did not seem fair that the exhibitors should make all the money. Even though Essanay were selling hundreds of copies of my films, they were selling them along old-fashioned lines of distribution. Sydney suggested scaling the larger theatres according to their seating capacity. With this plan each film could increase the receipts to a hundred thousand dollars or more. Anderson thought this was impossible; it would butt up against the policy of the whole Motion Picture Trust, involving sixteen thousand theatres, whose rules and methods of buying pictures were irrevocable; few exhibitors would pay such terms.

Later the *Motion Picture Herald* announced that the Essanay Company had discarded its old method of selling and, as Sydney had suggested, was scaling its terms according to the seating capacity of a theatre. This, as Sydney said it would, upped the receipts a hundred thousand dollars on each of my comedies. This news made me prick up my ears. Getting only twelve hundred and fifty dollars a week and doing all the work of writing, acting, and directing, I began to complain that I was working too hard and that I needed more time to make my pictures. I had a year's contract and had been turning out comedies every two to three weeks. Action soon came from Chicago; Spoor hopped a train to Los Angeles and as an extra inducement made an agreement to give me a ten-thousand-dollar bonus with each picture. With this stimulus my health improved.

About this time D. W. Griffith produced his epic, *The Birth of a Nation*, which made him the outstanding director of motion pictures. He undoubtedly was a genius of the silent cinema. Though his work was melodramatic and at times outré and absurd, Griffith's pictures had an original touch that made each one worth seeing.

De Mille started with great promise with *The Whispering Chorus* and a version of *Carmen*, but after *Male and Female* his work never went beyond the chemise and the boudoir. Nevertheless, I was so impressed with his *Carmen* that I made a two-reel burlesque of it, my last film with Essanay. After I had left them they put in all the cut-outs and extended it to four reels, which prostrated me and sent me to bed for two days. Although this was a dishonest act, it rendered a service, for thereafter I had it stipulated in every contract that there should be no mutilating, extending or interfering with my finished work.

The approaching end of my contract brought Spoor back to the coast with a proposition, he said, that no one could match. He would give me three hundred and fifty thousand dollars if I delivered him twelve two-reel pictures, he to pay the cost of production. I told him that on signing any contract I wanted one hundred and fifty thousand dollars' bonus plonked down first. This terminated any further talks with Spoor.

The future, the future—the wonderful future! Where was it leading? The prospects were dazzling. Like an avalanche, money and success came with increasing momentum; it was all bewildering, frightening—but wonderful.

*   *   *

While Sydney was in New York reviewing various offers, I was completing the filming of *Carmen* and living at Santa Monica in a house facing the sea. Some evenings I dined at Nat Goodwin's Café at the end of Santa Monica pier. Nat Goodwin was considered the greatest actor and light comedian on the American stage. He had had a brilliant career both as a Shakespearian actor and a modern light comedian. He was a close friend of Sir Henry Irving, and had married eight times, each wife being celebrated for her beauty. His fifth wife was Maxine Elliott, whom he whimsically referred to as 'the Roman Senator'. 'But she was beautiful and remarkably intelligent,' he said. He was an amiable cultured man, advanced in years, with a profound sense of humour; and now he had retired. Although I had never seen him act on the stage, I very much revered him and his great reputation.

We became very good friends and in the chill autumn

186

evenings we would walk along the deserted ocean front together. The drear melancholy atmosphere accentuated a glow to my inner excitement. When he heard that I was going to New York at the completion of my picture, he gave me some excellent advice. 'You've made a remarkable success, and there's a wonderful life ahead of you if you know how to handle yourself. . . . When you get to New York keep off Broadway, keep out of the public's eye. The mistake with many successful actors is that they want to be seen and admired—it only destroys the illusion.' His voice was deep and resonant. 'You'll be invited everywhere,' he continued, 'but don't accept. Pick out one or two friends and be satisfied to imagine the rest. Many a great actor has made the mistake of accepting every social invitation. John Drew was an example; he was a great favourite with society and went to all their houses, but they would not go to his theatre. They had had him in their drawing-rooms. You've captivated the world, and you can continue doing so if you stand outside it,' he said wistfully.

They were wonderful talks, rather sad, as we walked in the autumn twilight along the abandoned ocean front—Nat at the end of his career, I at the beginning of mine.

When I finished cutting *Carmen*, I hurriedly packed a small grip, and went directly from my dressing-room to the six o'clock train for New York, sending Sydney a telegram stating when I would leave and arrive.

It was a slow train which took five days to get there. I sat alone in an open compartment—in those days I was unrecognised without my comedy make-up. We were going the southern route through Amarillo, Texas, arriving there at seven in the evening. I had decided to shave, but other passengers were in the wash-room before me, so I had to wait. Consequently I was still in my underwear when we neared Amarillo. As we ploughed into the station, we were suddenly enveloped in babbling excitement. Peeking out of the wash-room window, I saw the station packed with a large milling crowd. Bunting and flags were wrapped and hung from pillar to post, and on the platform were several long tables set with refreshments. A celebration to welcome the arrival or departure of some local potentate, I thought. So I began to lather my face. But the excitement grew, then quite audibly I heard voices saying: 'Where is he?' Then a stampede entered the car, people running up and down the aisle shouting: 'Where is he? Where's Charlie Chaplin?'

'Yes?' I replied.

'On behalf of the Mayor of Amarillo, Texas, and all your fans, we invite you to have a drink and a light refreshment with us.'

I was seized with sudden panic. 'I can't, like this!' I said through shaving soap.

'Oh, don't bother about anything, Charlie. Just put on a dressing-gown and meet the folks.'

Hurriedly I washed my face, and, half-shaved, put on a shirt and tie and came out of the train buttoning my coat.

I was greeted with cheers. The mayor tried to speak: 'Mr Chaplin, on behalf of your fans of Amarillo——' but his voice was drowned by the continual cheering. He started again: 'Mr Chaplin, on behalf of your fans of Amarillo——' Then the crowd pressed forward, pushing the mayor into me and squashing us against the train, so that for a moment the welcoming speech was forgotten in quest of personal safety.

'Get back!' shouted the police, plunging through the crowd to make a way for us.

The Mayor lost his enthusiasm for the whole enterprise and spoke with slight asperity to the police and myself: 'All right, Charlie, let's get it over with, then you can get back on the train.'

After a general scramble to the tables, things quietened down and the mayor at last was able to make his address. He tapped the table with a spoon. 'Mr Chaplin, your friends of Amarillo, Texas, want to show their appreciation for all the happiness you have given them by asking you to join us in a sandwich and a Coca-Cola.'

After delivering his encomium, he asked if I would say a few words, urging me to get up on the table, where I mumbled something to the effect that I was happy to be in Amarillo and was so surprised by this wonderful, thrilling welcome that I would remember it for the rest of my life, etc. Then I sat down and tried to talk with the Mayor.

I asked him how he knew of my coming. 'Through the telegraph operators,' he said, explaining that the telegram I sent to Sydney had been relayed to Amarillo, then to Kansas City, Chicago and New York, and that the operators had given the news to the press.

When I returned to the train I sat meekly in my seat, my mind for the moment a blank. Then the whole car became a turbulence of people passing up and down the aisle, staring and giggling. What had taken place in Amarillo I could not mentally digest or properly enjoy. I was too excited, I just sat tense, elated and depressed all at the same time.

Several telegrams were handed to me before the train departed. Said one: 'Welcome, Charlie, we're waiting for you in Kansas City.' Another: 'There will be a limousine at your disposal when you arrive in Chicago to take you from one station to the other.' A third: 'Will you stay over for the night and be the guest of the Blackstone Hotel?' As we neared Kansas City, people stood along the side of the railroad track, shouting and waving their hats.

The large railroad station in Kansas City was packed solidly with people. The police were having difficulty controlling further crowds accumulating outside. A ladder was placed against the train to enable me to mount it and show myself on the roof. I found myself repeating the same banal words as in Amarillo. More telegrams awaited me: would I visit schools and institutions? I stuffed them in my suitcase, to be answered in New York. From Kansas City to Chicago people were again standing at railroad junctions and in fields, waving as the train swept by. I wanted to enjoy it all without reservation, but I kept thinking the world had gone crazy! If a few slapstick comedies could arouse such excitement, was there not something bogus about all celebrity? I had always thought I would like the public's attention, and here it was—paradoxically isolating me with a depressing sense of loneliness.

In Chicago, where it was necessary to change trains and stations, crowds lined the exit and hoorayed me into a limousine. I was driven to the Blackstone Hotel and given a suite of rooms to rest in before embarking for New York.

At the Blackstone a telegram awaited me from the Chief of Police of New York, requesting that I oblige him by getting off at 125th Street, instead of arriving at Grand Central Station as scheduled, as crowds were already gathering there in anticipation.

At 125th Street Sydney met me with a limousine, tense and excited. He spoke in whispers. 'What do you think of it?' he said. 'Crowds have been gathering from early morning at the station, and the press has been issuing bulletins every day since you left Los Angeles.' He showed me a newspaper announcing in big black type: 'He's here!' Another headline: 'Charlie in hiding!' On the way to the hotel he told me that he had completed a deal with the Mutual Film Corporation amounting to six hundred and seventy thousand dollars payable at ten thousand a week, and after I had passed the insurance test, a hundred and fifty thousand bonus would be paid on my signing the contract. He had a lunch engagement with the lawyer which would occupy him for the rest of the day, so he would drop me off at the Plaza, where he had booked a room for me, and would see me in the morning.

As Hamlet said: 'Now I am alone.' That afternoon I walked the streets and looked into shop windows and paused aimlessly on street corners. Now what happens to me? Here I was at the apogee of my career—all dressed up and no place to go. How does one get to know people, interesting people ? It seemed that everyone knew me, but I knew no one; I became introspective, full of self-pity, and a spell of melancholy beset me. I remember a successful Keystone comedian once saying: 'Now that we've arrived, Charlie, what's it all about?' 'Arrived where?' I answered.

I thought of Nat Goodwin's advice; 'Keep off Broadway.' Broadway was a desert as far as I was concerned. I thought of old friends whom I would like to meet framed in this success extravaganza—did I have old friends either in New York, London or elsewhere? I wanted a special audience—perhaps Hetty Kelly. I had not heard from her since my entry into movies—her reactions would be amusing.

She was then living in New York with her sister, Mrs Frank Gould. I took a walk up Fifth Avenue; 834 was her sister's address. I paused outside the house, wondering if she were there, but I had not the courage to call. However, she might come out and I could accidentally bump into her. I waited for about half an hour, sauntering up and down, but no one went in or came out of the house.

I went to Childs Restaurant at Columbus Circle and ordered wheat-cakes and a cup of coffee. I was served perfunctorily until I asked the waitress for an extra pat of butter; then she recognised me. From then on it was a chain reaction until every-one in the restaurant and from the kitchen was peering at me. Eventually I was obliged to propel my way through an immense crowd that had gathered both inside and out, and escape in a passing taxi.

For two days I walked about New York without meeting anyone I knew, vacillating between happy excitement and depression. Meanwhile the insurance doctors had examined me. A few days later, Sydney came to the hotel, elated. 'It's all settled, you've passed the insurance.'

The formalities of signing the contract followed. I was photo-graphed receiving the one-hundred-and-fifty-thousand-dollar cheque. That evening I stood with the crowd in Times Square as the news flashed on the electric sign that runs round the Times Building. It read: 'Chaplin signs with Mutual at six hundred and seventy thousand a year.' I stood and read it objectively as though it were about someone else. So much had happened to me, my emotions were spent.